INSIDE
Facebook

Life, Work and Visions of Greatness

Karel M. Baloun
Senior Engineer, Facebook Inc., 2005-2006

Note for Librarians: A cataloguing record for this book is available from Library and Archives Canada at www.collectionscanada.ca/amicus/index-e.html

ISBN 1-4251-1300-1

Trafford's print shop runs on "green energy" from solar, wind and other environmentally-friendly power sources.

PUBLISHING™

Offices in Canada, USA, Ireland and UK

Book sales for North America and international:
Trafford Publishing, 6E–2333 Government St.,
Victoria, BC V8T 4P4 CANADA
phone 250 383 6864 (toll-free 1 888 232 4444)
fax 250 383 6804; email to orders@trafford.com

Book sales in Europe:
Trafford Publishing (UK) Limited, 9 Park End Street, 2nd Floor
Oxford, UK OX1 1HH UNITED KINGDOM
phone +44 (0)1865 722 113 (local rate 0845 230 9601)
facsimile +44 (0)1865 722 868; info.uk@trafford.com

Order online at:
trafford.com/06-3059

10 9 8 7 6 5 4 3 2

As an early engineer, I was on the inside during Facebook's explosive growth. In *Inside Facebook,* I'll give you the scoop on the company as it became the premiere online environment for U.S. college students, including how and by whom the products were made, how you can use them best, views on what makes social networks so valuable, and where the industry is headed. You, too, can achieve startup success and attain your greatest dream; I hope to inspire you toward fulfilling your potential.

Cover: Michael Hughes
(mike_hughes3@yahoo.com).

Orders, inquiries and information regarding the digital edition: http://www.fbbook.com or karel@fbbook.com

I've found something to put here. Now it's <u>your turn</u>.

Cast of Characters

Zuck—creator of "A Mark Zuckerberg Production"

Dustin—CTO, right-hand man

Matt—VP of whatever is needed the most

Owen—COO

Sean—President

Jeff—possessor of all technical answers

TS—all engineers directly reported to him

Ezra and Noah—Product (yes, all of it)

Kent—Ads

Scott, D'Angelo, Victor, Andrew, James, Taner, Nick, and Aaron —initial tech team

Steve Chen—founder of YouTube, in a rare cameo appearance.

I've found something to put here. Now it's <u>your turn</u>.

Introduction

Facebook is No. 1 in the amount of time spent on-site by visiting users.[1] Think about that. A site that didn't even exist three years ago is *the* place on the Internet where visiting users spend more time than on any other site. Facebook is the most important site for folks in college. Facebook is the most successful privately held, closed social network.[2] Facebook is also a first job for many of the people who work there, and a once-in-a-lifetime experience for everyone else.

As one of the first engineers hired, I quickly found myself deep inside Facebook. I was in my thirties with ten years of

---

1 According to ComScore's MediaMetrix, early 2006. Since a few other sites have more visitors than Facebook it isn't the site where the most total time is spent, but it is high in the top ten.

2 MySpace launched between September 2003 and January 2004, a year before Facebook and about the same time as Friendster, and has both more members and more pageviews. Friendster was once near dead, and the word is that this was because Jonathan Abrams hates his users, or at least loves his own ideas about his site's feature set more. He has since departed. Also, it became huge in the Philippines, which is not easily monetizable traffic. Alexa.com says Friendster is back into the top thirty U.S. Web sites, back from its dive out of the top 150, and up 64 percent in daily usage over the last three months. But I often can't even get to the site. All Friendster has at this point is an interesting patent (http://www.redherring.com/Article.aspx?a=17498&hed=Friendster +Wins+Patent), so I have pretty much ignored them here. In this book, I discuss at length whether MySpace or Facebook is more successful. In short, I believe Facebook has deeper utility.

I've found something to put here. Now it's <u>your turn</u>.

Internet engineering experience, and suddenly I felt like an old man.

When I was in college, there was no popular Internet and just fifty Web sites, perhaps three people were limited to using Archie and Usenet to share porn. I played the original Oregon Trail, which is now relegated to this popular Facebook joke group.[3] I didn't know what I wanted do with my life. It's a good thing, too, I guess, because the thing I'd end up doing didn't exist yet. So, in writing this book, I bring the Engineer and Old Fart perspectives.

At Facebook, the product people and the engineers got along well together because we sat right next to each other and were all building the site together. The engineers did more coding and the product people did more writing, but we were constantly thinking about what our users would want and how things should work. Whatever we worked on was ours and we really cared about it.

This passion and commitment, and so many other things about Facebook, are unique, even in Silicon Valley, so I decided that you should know about them. Facebook has already changed so many lives, so many relationships; it has become an integral part of college life. With the release and widespread adoption of its developer API,[4] Facebook will

---

3 http://www.facebook.com/group.php?gid=2200179695

4 http://developers.facebook.com

I've found something to put here. Now it's your turn.

cement its position as a key social networking service in the web 2.0 landscape.[5]

In Inside Facebook, I will describe how a successful social network was built, how it compares to other similar services, and how I see the social Internet landscape developing. But first, I'll tell you how Facebook was born and how I and some others got started with it. It's the kind of dream that can come true for anyone. I'll let you in on the secret.[6]

My style here is to constantly weave three threads: the Facebook story, my personal experiences in Silicon Valley, and details about the social Internet industry. I will bounce around a bit, so if you get dizzy just take a break, look off into the distance, and pull on one of those anti-nausea accupressure bands[7] like my wife does.

---

5 http://www.go2web20.net/

6 http://www.fbbook.com/p.php?p=secret&s=1

7 http://www.amazon.com/exec/obidos/ASIN/B0001AFM0W/ptradescom-20

Go do. Build your idea. Share for help.

(By the way, here is my own rendition of Pokey the Hedgehog in commemoration of his murder, sadly before he was given a chance to show his true potential. By paying careful attention to Matt's contributions, diligent readers will be richly rewarded with knowledge of Pokey's life.)

A Year in the Life of a Yopo[8]

On April 21, 2005, I got a seemingly ignorable email via
LinkedIn.com:

> Hi Karel,
> I'm VP and GM at Thefacebook, the top site for
> college students in the US. [...] Given your
> experience at LookSmart, I thought you might be a
> good fit. Thefacebook is still a very small team
> despite having a strong market position, so this is
> a great opportunity for the right person. If you're
> interested in talking with us please let me know the
> best way to get in touch with you.
> Thanks,
> Matt

Thus started a yearlong dreamlike odyssey, from which I have
just awoken.

A few quick weeks later I was one of the first ten engineers,
papers signed on May 5, 2005. I may have been engineer
number seven or nine, depending on how many informal
contributions we acknowledge. Nevertheless, preceding me
clearly are only Zuck himself, Dustin the Man, D'Angelo the
Brain, Victor, James, Aaron, and McCollum. To bring
experience to a code base of which every line had been written
by someone younger than twenty, two other senior engineers,
Steve Chen and Scott, were hired with me. Scott has a Master's

---

8 Young professional. This term was invented by Noah Kagan.

I've found something to put here. Now it's <u>your turn</u>.

degree in computer science and immediately attacked one
difficult problem after another; within four months of hiring
he had singlehandedly built most of the Internet's largest
photo sharing Web site. Steve, an early engineer at Paypal, was
often hard to locate, and left within a couple of months. Yet,
even Steve made it big; he immediately co-founded YouTube.[9]

The message of the YouTube story is similar to this tale of
Facebook. A twenty-six-year-old during the short time he was
at Facebook, Steve was looking at two choices: be a critical
early engineer at a succeeding startup (again, since he'd done
that before at Paypal) or start his own company with his buddy
Chad. He had just bought a wildly overpriced condo in San
Francisco with his girlfriend and they enjoyed weekend days
furnishing it. But when I talked to him about the risks of
adjustable rate mortgages and how he should maybe stick
with Facebook because it was a guaranteed paycheck, since
having negative equity in your home can lead to bankruptcy,
his mind was obviously somewhere else. His vision had him
worth millions. His fearless and doubt-free focus was on
creating value and trusting that the money would follow. The
details of his mortgages would be handled by financial
servants. Since only sixteen months later YouTube is selling to
Google for $1.65 billion, I laugh to myself at how insistent we
were that he personally return his corporate laptop!

---

9 The leading video sharing site. Alexa ranked it the nineteenth "most
popular" site in the United States in June 2006, right below Facebook's
rank of seventeen.

Go do. Build your idea. Share for help.

My being introduced to Facebook through LinkedIn fits on so many levels. LinkedIn is the closest we thirty-somethings have to online social networking. I'd been using that site for over a year to gain and maintain business relationships, naturally. Like most anyone over twenty-five I had never heard of the Facebook, and like most engineers in Silicon Valley, I hear regularly about new opportunities. The three reasons I didn't ignore this email were Matt Cohler's incredible talent for selling the dream of Facebook, the fact that my good friend David Kopp was the LinkedIn referrer, and the fact that he sent me a concurrent email telling me to take the job or else.

After me came a quick infusion of brilliant summer interns: Tiankai "Tank" Liu, Charles "La" La, and Darian Shirazi,[10] who contributed hundreds of code commits before even getting into college.

As I get off the Facebook boat following my adventure there, I notice that everyone who started the journey with me has succeeded in their own way. Scott[11] is now the most trusted technologist/engineer at Facebook, a well deserved right hand man to Dustin, who's grown into a capable and authoritative CTO. Victor, James, and Aaron continue to make key

---

10 In perhaps the longest running interpersonal gag, Darian was always getting fired by Dustin.

11 http://www.facebook.com/profile.php?id=210081

I've found something to put here. Now it's your turn.

contributions.[12] D'Angelo graduated from Caltech and McCollum is finishing up at Harvard next year. I'm sure both have a stack of job offers, and D'Angelo is now the brand new CTO, cementing youth in the key positions of the company. Since Steve left very few traces of code during his short sojourn, every time I heard "we hired Karel and Steve for their experience" I didn't take it as a good sign.

How I Got In and How You Can, Too

My interviews were . . . unconventional. I first spoke to Matt at around 10 p.m. on the night I replied to the LinkedIn email. That was my phone interview. It mostly consisted of his masterful presentation on why Facebook would become what it is today. He was so good I offered to come interview that night. Matt said they work late, after all.[13] Turned out Zuck was going to be at UC Berkeley the next day, so we agreed to meet for an interview over lunch at Naan 'N' Curry on Telegraph Avenue. Matt arranged it all by shouting at Zuck

---

12 Victor recently led a re-architecture of the code base to standardize on object types; James has rewritten the Groups, Message, Invite, and Events features at least three times each; and Aaron does many front end implementations, including for Social Map and the NCAA tournament.

13 Little could I have imagined how late.

Go do. Build your idea. Share for help.

across the room. It was decided in less than a minute; I felt that kind of culture was for me.[14]

I really did call Mark "Zuck" in those days when I reported to him, spoke to him regularly, and shared long, meaningful IM chats in the middle of the night. Now people call him Mark, usually with a shake or quaver in the speaker's voice. But this book is about the spirit of the early Facebook, and he was certainly Zuck then.

Matt is rightfully proud of the recruiting metric he devised, so I'll share it with you. He said that the Facebook had the highest pageview-to-engineer ratio on the planet, ever. At the time, Facebook was serving over a billion pageviews a month for 4 million users, and Facebook had less than ten engineers. Amazing. I could release a change that would immediately be seen by more people than the entire city of Los Angeles. And if I believe the fallacy[15] that all engineers are created equal,

---

14 Noah says, "Many decisions happened in hallways, bathrooms, and at other random times. It was a nice environment not having to wait for a scheduled meeting but to just grab the right person and make things happen.

15 In reality, a small fraction of engineers are the most productive in any given organization. Paul Graham writes about this in Hackers and Painters and, less directly in the context of describing real hackers, online (http://paulgraham.com/gh.html). A Facebook example: Over a couple of months Scott almost singlehandedly wrote most of the photos application, which by itself represents a significant percentage of the site's pageviews and is the leading photo sharing site on the Internet.

I've found something to put here. Now it's your turn.

my personal share of pageviews served is 100 million pages per month. Insane!

I was eager to meet Zuck. In retrospect, it's odd that I didn't know what he looked like, and I spent my waiting minutes guessing how a twenty-year-old CEO would look. Had I been a bit smarter I would have used Facebook to learn something about him. It's amazing that I never thought of that, but that is how foreign a social networking application was to a thirty-three-year-old. I did check out a random profile, though, to learn how the application itself worked. I studied the software without even thinking to just use it!

In retrospect I guess I was lucky that Zuck chose to ask technical-puzzle-type analytical questions to test my skill and intelligence. I thought that my Masters degree in social psychology and years of Internet experience would make me a lightening quick study on the social uses of the Internet. Not true.

After we chatted about my technical experience, Zuck asked his first question, something about sorting a list with only one temporary variable. I only did okay, though I got through it. Maybe there was a mix up in his phrasing the problem in a way that made it impossible to solve. I could tell that I hadn't fully satisfied him on the most critical part of the entire interview process. So I made the best interview decision of my life: I decide to go double or nothing. "Why don't you give me another one?" I asked "Ok, I think I will," he said. And while the

Go do. Build your idea. Share for help.

excitement of answering that one perfectly completely blocks out my memory of what exactly the question was, I knew that I had satisfied him. I left the interview delighted at my new opportunity to really make a difference in the lives of so many people.

A day or two later my offer arrived through the fax. I signed almost immediately, on May 5, 2005, I think. Within another day or two I was working nights, getting oriented, and reading code while tying up loose ends at LookSmart. The excitement was completely natural: coding Facebook was the most exciting thing I could be doing, so why not start right away.

So, that's how I got in the door. After I give you a tour of life in the early office, I'll tell you how others got started with Facebook, giving you clues as to how you can locate your dream startup, too.

Facebook now occupies its second formal office, right off of the Stanford campus on University Avenue.[16] The current building is slick and smart—exactly what you'd imagine for a successful Internet company. The first Facebook office, the place I landed at around the corner on Emerson Street, was unlike any other.

---

16 Noah says, "Right above the bead shop, which is a great place to meet women, and across from the delicious Miyake. My response: Noah doesn't know Japanese food. But that's okay; I don't know women. Better to go to Sushi Ya a few blocks down on the right.

I've found something to put here. Now it's <u>your turn</u>.

Working in Facebook's First Office

In a plain white building above a Chinese restaurant was a smallish office space with three small rooms with actual doors, three smaller storage rooms that functioned as close-able offices, and a 20 ft. by 35 ft. room with a table taking up most of it that served as a conference room. These rooms surrounded a central open area (maybe 40 ft. by 100 ft.), about a quarter of which was a makeshift reception area. The rest was . . . everything. In that space, in which a person could not walk more than ten steps without hitting a wall, worked about a dozen people.

The key principle that made this possible was that no one had any of "their own" space except the few enshrined in offices— Sean, the President, the summer interns, and Operations in the persons of Taner H[17] and Nick Heyman. Zuck would come into the office and, seeing every chair full, just lie down on the thin carpet on his belly, sandals flapping, and start typing into his little white Mac iBook. Each of the two small tables had four 24-inch LCD monitors that pointed outward to form a square in the middle of the table, leaving room for four keyboards facing each chair and not much else. In the center behind the monitors was a garbage can, or the place where very important papers were collected from around the office

17 Halicioglu. Even after a year, I can't spelled it right; Just now I cribbed it from my Facebook Friends list. He understands server hardware and operations troubleshooting better than anyone I know.

Go do. Build your idea. Share for help.

and gently deposited. I'm not sure which. Along with food wrappers and empty cans, I'd often find my notes and important mail for Zuck in that can. This was my first hint that I ought to evolve beyond trying to keep paper notes.

Notice anything interesting in this picture of me from that time? It's obviously nothing having to do with me. Nice paint job on the back wall, eh? From the well-endowed lady on the cow in the entry stairwell, to something that needed to be painted over in the ladies room before I ever saw it— and before we hired some ladies—just about every wall was

I've found something to put here. Now it's <u>your turn</u>.

painted with <u>blueish-metallic graffiti</u>.[18] You can also see the nice chair that we assembled ourselves, and some typical computer clutter on the floor.

I had been using a Linux desktop for five years but switched to an Apple OS X laptop after I started. The company is divided about evenly between PCs and Mac laptops. In the beginning, McCollum had a desktop tower, maybe to secure his physical space in the open office! At first there weren't enough chairs so it was better to arrive early in the day. Once the nice chairs arrived, we all assembled our own, just like they did at the early eBay. Of course there were no phones. There still are no personal land line phones. We used IM heavily and some email, though most interoffice communication was handled just by being in the same space, especially at night.

The huge refrigerator was stocked by shopping trips to Safeway thanks to one of the office helpers[19] or even Zuck's very <u>nice girlfriend</u>[20] at the time. It was loaded with various cool caffeinated drinks, and commenced my nine-month addiction, finally broken, to those little bottled Starbucks

---

18 <u>http://harvard.facebook.com/photo.php?</u>
<u>pid=30785563&id=10030226</u>

19 All really nice girls, like Jennifer (whose profile I can't find since we no longer share a network. See, there are limits.) and Krysia.(<u>http://</u>
<u>www.facebook.com/profile.php?id=200151</u>)

20 <u>http://berkeley.facebook.com/profile.php?id=1202422</u>

Go do. Build your idea. Share for help.

coffee drinks.[21] I made one shopping run to the nearby Whole Foods to create a Tea Bar, which remained consistently untouched. The Odwallas I bought were consumed within hours, but their expense exceeded even the generosity of the pre-office-manager Facebook.

Unfortunately there was only one couch at the time, and besides being well used at night, it was also in the game room, where late at night a few engineers could be found playing on the Xbox console. I was woken up at around 4 a.m. one morning by Sean asking if I could drive him home (to the place he shared with Zuck and Dustin, whose pre-VC car I also once jumped). I think his car got impounded since he couldn't organize having both a license and insurance at the same time, even with an assistant's help. Sean is like that: extremely valuable as a visionary, idea driver, and cheerleader—he gave Facebook much credibility at a time when the company might not have been able to continue without him—but he's even more scattered on practical matters than me, which says a lot.

Through the couch room, one could get to another essential work area of the early office: the roof. Climbing up on a table and shimmying out a tall, thin window, we could enjoy about 300 square gravelly feet of fresh air, equipped with an handful of laid back wood-and-cloth pool chairs. Of course, we had

---

21 Broken by the best tasting hot chocolate in the Bay Area. I have replaced it with an addiction to the finest Venezuelan Abuelo (http://www.coupacafe.com/ourstores.html).

I've found something to put here. Now it's your turn.

wireless Internet so could take our laptops anywhere we wanted. It was a beautiful early summer in California—bright, blue skies but no hotter than was comfortable. It turns out that a Powerbook has just enough backlighting to be useable while wearing sunglasses. And the roof was the only place you could make phone calls without bothering every engineer in the company. I conducted many telephone interviews out there, or during my daily commute.[22] One day Zuck fell asleep on the roof and came in a few hours later with an impressive sunburn. Facebook's original product manager Ezra, who might one day stop requesting deferrals and actually go to law school, also loved to work out there and developed a fine tan.

Within my first month, the atmosphere of the office was dramatically upgraded with the hiring of Susie, who somehow got everything organized and has been a stable rock at every stage of the company's growth.

Around the end of May 2005, Zuck painted the word "Forsan" on his office wall in huge letters, and used it as his Facebook picture for a few days. The word comes from Virgil's *Aeneid*: "Forsan et haec olim meminisse iuvabit," which can be loosely translated to read "Perhaps, one day, even this will seem pleasant to remember". Zuck has a flair for personal dramatics, mimicking the pose of the statue of Father Junipero

---

22 My commute was sixty to ninety minutes each way. That's long, even by Bay Area standards, and genuinely reflected my enthusiasm for the opportunity.

Go do. Build your idea. Share for help.

Serra and equating his foray into the social networking space to the launch of Virgil's voyage.

The first day I walked into the office, I saw Zuck and Sean together for the first time.

Zuck was wearing his Apollo shirt, a low key basketball jersey with the name Apollo and a large "1" on the back, and both men had curly golden locks from the bright summer sunshine. The thought briefly swam through my head that, in appearance and confidence, they looked like prototypical Greek gods, like the statues I saw touring the Parthenon. The thought was rapidly replace by others, and no, I'm not gay.

Zuck also had fun with his position. He had two sets of business cards printed: on one his title was "CEO." On the other, it said "I'm the CEO . . . bitch!"[23] By the way, did you know that you can decorate a birthday cake with a perfectly printed image of a Web page? Zuck discovered this at his all-hands birthday party.

---

23 Jerry Yang labeled himself Chief Yahoo.

I've found something to put here. Now it's <u>your turn</u>.

How You Can Find Your Startup Dream

To be in your own wildly successful startup, you either need to build it yourself or find the right one in its infancy.

Finding one, the right startup, requires luck and judgment. Obviously I had plenty of luck on my side, since Facebook contacted me. But, as they say, luck favors the prepared: I was a heavy user of LinkedIn. The judgment part was easy for me: Since Facebook was already so hot at many colleges, it was obvious to me that it would win at the rest of them. May you have it so easy.

Here are some key ideas:

- Everyone at Facebook before me knew Zuck well. The lesson is: Stick with your brilliant friends and encourage them to succeed!

- Since you can only attend to a finite number of brilliant friends, choose wisely. If someone you know has what looks to you like a powerful idea, figure out how you can help drive it forward with whatever amount of time and energy you can contribute.

- Once you are engaged and things are looking good, become indispensable. What a founder most needs is completely trustworthy, effective implementers, people who can read his mind because they know him so well. So much work

Go do. Build your idea. Share for help.

needs doing to push out a new company, whichever of the founders' thoughts you can implement well is precious. Your own thoughts about what the company should do are probably just a distraction.

- Be flexible. Become good at whatever it is that needs doing most. Young people are absolutely the best at this and it could be your unique advantage.[24] Dustin has been Zuck's right-hand man from the earliest dorm room days. He grew the site to all colleges, along the way learning everything he needed to know, like programming and technology, to scale the site.

- Do it. Don't talk about it or question it. Just do. A startup needs too much done too fast, in whatever way.

"Just do it" can mean a countless number of things, as it is only the results derived from the attitude that matter. It means quickly choosing a path and not getting distracted until the

---

24 We old guys are screwed (http://www.nytimes.com/2006/07/31/business/31men.html). Seriously, only those eager to adapt will get back in. Perhaps this makes us more likely to choose the "build it" rather than the "join it" option, but I haven't seen evidence that we are more likely to succeed at building it. If anything, I'd guess that success is correlated to the number of well-attempted failures, and even the thirty-somethings who've worked at corporations for many, many years may not have attempted any. Paul Graham quotes Zod Nazem, chief of Yahoo engineering, as saying he'd rather hire someone who's tried their own startup and failed than a corporate engineering worker bee. (See http://www.paulgraham.com/hiring.html and http://dondodge.typepad.com/the_next_big_thing/2005/09/the_innovators_.html)

I've found something to put here. Now it's <u>your turn</u>.

job is done. It means not endlessly asking around about how to do it, but just doing it as you think best. This leaves little time for perfectionism. Your passion and attitude are key; reasonable people understand the practical limits, especially around time and busyness.

So, which one of the hundreds of ideas your dozens of friends generate is the next billion dollar company? The first test is passion. Your friend will become convinced that his idea is big, and will be putting all of his or her life energy into it, or into parts related to it. Zuck actually came to Palo Alto to breathe life into Wirehog, a network file sharing system that he had come up with. But he was still intensely passionate about Facebook, so even if you had tagged along with him for Wirehog, you'd still end up working on a winning product.

The second test is big vision in a few small steps. An idea has to become a big deal without taking much time or requiring a lot of work. Even complex ideas must start as a single, simple project that can easily be understood and finished. It is a good sign if the "idea ladder" from the simple idea to the big vision is well worked out. It is a bad sign if the leader isn't clear on what to finish first or what "finished" looks like.[25]

---

25 Noah says, "I disagree. If you had created Google, could you have explained it from the beginning, before searching became the norm? I think the idea is more about creating something that is truly unique and immediately useful."

Go do. Build your idea. Share for help.

The third test is the immediate and energetic support of others who are involved. While some artists are never understood in their own time, popular Web sites usually experience early success, and at least a core of supporters who really understand and can share the vision, as with digg.com or reddit.com. Habitual nay-sayers and other losers are present everywhere to criticize and tear down creative ideas. They can be filtered out and ignored. But respected voices who believe in the idea should be involved in some way. The idea leader may have trouble involving others—everyone is busy—but if you are the earliest partner on an idea, remember that you are probably not the first person who's heard the pitch. Think about why everyone else wasn't excited. Facebook was popular at Harvard from its very first day. Its eventual success was evident immediately. It was providing personal, detailed, timely and valuable information that would never appear on Google or Wikipedia. So, for me making my job decision, the value of Facebook was immediately clear, validated by millions of passionate members.

Some successful sites such as eBay needed time or product changes to get big, so if you were considering to join such a company at its beginning, the decision is complex. But such a decision doesn't need to be made until it is easier, since you can follow the company keeping your connections, until immediately after that corner is turned. Then pour in your energy.

I've found something to put here. Now it's <u>your turn</u>.

The fourth test is low user churn and increasing usage per user. Do users of the site tend to become more involved and more attached to the site over time, or do they drift off. If existing users love the site, you can tell by examining their actual site usage patterns. They are likely to spend more time at and invest more energy into the site. If they do that, then other like-minded users will follow. Two-thirds of Facebook's members return every day, a startling statistic that has been true since its inception. On the other hand, another useful content site where millions of subscription magazine articles are available for free, Findarticles.com,[26] seems like an amazing idea. Yet it is not an extremely powerful site, because it immediately leaks away the vast majority of its search-engine-referred users. If you are thinking about working on a site with high churn, figure out how to solve that problem first, or keep active on other ideas until it is solved.

Some other factors you can more or less ignore. Facebook was already financially stable when I arrived, but whether the site is making money or not only matters relative to how long the site can continue to exist at its current level of spending. So if you want to join a startup, go to a place where there are a lot of them and get to know—and know well—the people who are creating them, while looking for the big winner or while working on your own idea on the side. Strategic thinking like

---

26 http://findarticles.com

Go do. Build your idea. Share for help.

this will increase your chances of finding the next Facebook-sized opportunity.

You Really Can Achieve Anything

One person can make a tremendous impact. That individual can be anyone, whether they have technical skills, business savvy, or some combination of the two. Especially you, wherever and whoever you are.

"Alright Karel, so then why aren't you Zuck? Why aren't you a billionaire, you lame hypocrite?" Ow! Could you please think that thought more quietly? Well, I did lack talent in key areas, and I didn't have an Internet growing up. Most significantly, though, I never dreamed of becoming a CEO by age twenty-one. I did dream about becoming an author once I'd collected some experiences. Only lately am I learning the art of practical dreaming, where I actually define the steps I need to take toward my dreams.[27]

Building a Web site is easier than ever, the barriers have come way down. Facebook was Zuck's third or fourth attempt at building a Web site, as you'll read below. My Facebook product friend Noah has built a few Web sites. Even I have one out and a few more in the works. It seems like everyone has

---

27 Now my dream is to rebuild society on equitable and ecologically sound foundations so global peace and cultural diversity blossom. I'll get back to you in ten years on that one.

I've found something to put here. Now it's <u>your turn</u>.

their own blog, and content management systems like Joomla, Mambo, Postnuke, Plone, and others or hosted site-creation systems like Ning, make even complex sites less difficult.[28] Ruby on Rails and PHP are much easier to learn and prototype quickly than Java/JSP or Perl/ModPerl/Mason. Bandwidth and hosting are cheap, easily under $50/month. A technically savvy kid could put together a nice Web site in days or weeks, and a software engineer or two can build a complex site in a few months.

So, anyone and their cousin seems to be building a site that they say is a Web 2.0 social site, because that's what is hot today. Seven years ago everyone was building a portal for this or that audience. Two years ago everyone had a blog with a twist. Now even magazines and stores want their own "social network," because, frankly, who wouldn't want to have[29] and operate a growing social network!

If you want to build your own startup, it comes down to having a powerful idea, building it out to completion, and marketing it right.[30] None of these essential steps are easy. Building a

---

28 http://joomla.org/, http://mamboserver.com/, http://postnuke.com,/, http://plone.org/, http://ning.com/

29 http://www.rev2.org/archives/2006/07/11/33-places-to-hangout-in-the-social-networking-era/

30 Noah says, "More important than the idea is having good execution. I can't even count how many ideas I have heard from friends, but I can count how many have done them. Zero."

Go do. Build your idea. Share for help.

site out as a prototype is easier than choosing the right idea to build out, especially if the idea is simple enough. As the web matures, though, and while the tools get better, the good ideas that haven't already been done become progressively harder. Building it right, so that it runs fast, doesn't lose data, and scales to millions of users, is still hard. But that kind of good engineering is easier to buy if the site concept is proven to work.

To find an idea, Noah suggests you think about something people do for thirty minutes a day that frustrates them[31] and see if you can automate it or cut the time they have to spend on it in half. What other mind games can we think of to identify easily doable services that would save people a lot of time and effort?

Perhaps the most difficult choice for an entrepreneur to make is deciding when to give up on an idea that is failing. Let's say you're running with a startup idea that hits a big roadblock, like no one coming to your completed site no matter what you do.[32] Along comes another exciting idea from another friend, another corner of your brain, or from the second position on

---

31 http://okdork.com/2006/03/20/noahs-secret-to-making-1-million-dollars/

32 http://ptrades.com

I've found something to put here. Now it's your turn.

your own list of exciting ideas to try. I'd <u>bet you</u>[33] that too many people[34] simply give up too soon.

Instead, try this:

Once you commit to an idea,[35] force yourself to make a list of actions that you promise to complete before giving up. Then just work your way through that list, satisfied simply that you are taking action and making progress. This strategy will force you to get through the inevitable setbacks and challenges that make startups worthwhile. Fold only once you've kept all the promises you made to yourself, convinced that your idea really wasn't good enough. Remember that you'll have to apologize to everyone who gifted their time, money, and energy to your cause.[36] If it were psychologically easy to force yourself

---

33 http://bet-u.com

34 Most notably for me are those folks named me, myself, and I

35 Carefully analyze whether the idea is worthwhile before you commit to it. This book is taking a ton of time to write, time that my wife and children would just love to have, and, gee, right now I feel I'd love to give it to them. But, instead, I've committed myself to finishing it. Only you, dear reader, can judge whether my time was well-spent.

36 Those who care about you or will continue to be important to you will forgive you. If you gave it your all you must have learned enough to make everything worthwhile—to all of you. Your next idea won't be any easier to complete, but you will have successfully struck out once. The number of times you get knocked down doesn't count, only the number of times you get back up. A young man goes up to a business guru and asks, "How can I become like you?" The wise man answers, "By making right decisions." "Oh, wise guru," the young man asks, "how do I do that?" "By making wrong decisions."

Go do. Build your idea. Share for help.

though the inevitable rejections and setbacks, *everyone* would be an Internet millionaire.

How do you build a successful site in a garage or dorm room? Take the most simple part of your idea and prototype it as quickly as possible. Next, show it to your intended audience and see if it sticks.

Don't just listen to feedback, watch what people actually do on your site. Watch how passionately they use it. See whether it is really solving the problem you intended to solve for your audience. Odds are you won't succeed on your first try. But wait! Don't give up on your original idea to solve a different problem for the same audience. Can you find a more appropriate audience? Actively modify your site until it accomplishes what you intended, and then monitor what works.[37]

Beyond the numbers, look at your key relationships with your core users and business or technology partners: Are your most important people getting more excited and passionate? Are you building enough of the right relationships to get your ball

---

37 You must track usage and use patterns, otherwise you are flying completely blind. You can write your own code for this, as Facebook did, or use one of any number of services: statcounter.com, google.com/analytics, coremetrics.com, onestat.com/html/servicesS2M.html, etc.

I've found something to put here. Now it's your turn.

rolling? Remember, <u>the rock to which you are clinging</u>[38] is your original vision. Keep your passion focused on that.

Lastly, how do you define "a successful Web site"? Is it simply becoming widely used and very popular, ideally with only a small investment of your life-span (like digg.com, which sits at No. 24 on the Alexa list of U.S. sites by popularity about a year and a half after its initial launch)?

Is it being tremendously rich and profitable, like Microsoft, Dell, or <u>Wal-Mart</u>,[39] all the while telling yourself that this is because you produce excellent products at an amazing value? Quickly transforming yourself into a free-market liberal economist, you'd argue that the market has correctly estimated your value and your profits are simply a reflection of how much more valuable you are to your customers than is the competition. Naturally, if the competition were as good as you, you'd have to lower your price and profit. Sure, and Bill Gates is really the Easter Bunny.

---

38 <u>http://www.lyricsfreak.com/e/enya/how+can+i+keep+from +singing_20050588.html</u>

39 Mallwart has cheap prices by lowering wages here and throughout the world, while its leadership, the members of the Walton family, occupy four spots on the Forbes billionaire Top 20 list. (See <u>http:// www.amazon.com/exec/obidos/ASIN/B000BTH4K4/ptradescom-20</u>, <u>http://carryabigsticker.com/mall_wart.htm</u>, <u>http://www.aflcio.org/ aboutus/thisistheaflcio/publications/magazine/walmart.cfm</u>,, <u>http:// www.benjaminedwards.net/Writings/walmart%20cap.htm</u>)

Go do. Build your idea. Share for help.

Is it some combination of popularity and real user value, estimated in some highly qualitative fashion, from how much you mean to users and how much they love you? Wikipedia and eBay probably score high here among their large and loyal user base. <u>Or is it something else?</u>[40] Perhaps it's just the feeling that you've done well, empowered others to be more than they thought possible, made your small group of friends happy, or even just got your creative ideas out?

Pardon me? Oh, all right. Here's more about how Facebook accomplished the creation of its site.

Building a Site Without Tools or Controls

Product engineering at the first office was an extremely simple process, and the few all-engineering meetings we had (a dozen people in the small conference room) were focused on keeping development fast and flexible. There existed the all important server "maverick," and

- All developers logged in as root to change code, directly used to serve the Harvard site.

- Occasionally we broke the site.

- But we immediately fixed it.

---

40 <u>http://www.fbbook.com/fblog/something-else</u>

I've found something to put here. Now it's <u>your turn</u>.

· A push script that would copy the Harvard program files to all of the other schools Facebook served.

The site had over 2.5 million members at the time, and well over a billion pageviews per month. Yet there was no source control and code changes were all made as root. That was okay as long as Dustin was making most of the changes. Actually, Dustin continued making most of the changes for a long, long time. Nick's first major Ops new hire, Dan Neff (who cooks an awesome BBQ and also set the Facebook commute record by driving daily almost two hours from out past Gilroy), within a few weeks put in Subversion source control, Trac for documentation, and a custom browser-based push script.

This direct development system worked amazingly well, even up to a half a dozen engineers. We used it until the first complete revamp of the site, called Project Facelift, which required source control for coordination among every new, old, and temporary engineer.

During these months I was feeling Experienced. Issues would arise for which I had the answers because the site was still comparable in size to others I'd worked on and actual Internet application experience was a rare commodity in the building. Jeff Rothschild (technical guru and founder of Veritas) came on shortly after I did, and very soon he was providing all the answers. Jeff's arrival made it clear that Facebook could not fail and I loved working for someone as technically talented.

Go do. Build your idea. Share for help.

I mapped out the first system diagrams and planned a major architectural redesign for PHP5. Around four months in, Zuck gave my favorite engineering roadmap presentation, in which he assigned me to about half of the site's code base and features. After the meeting, he walked directly up to me and kindly asked if he had given enough attention to my items. That's Zuck—always concerned that everyone who is working for him is happy, as long as they are important. I was managing a team of over half a dozen engineers building a valuable product. I was in love and every day was a delight. At the time, every day, I acknowledged that this was one of the best work times of my life; my gratitude magnified my joyfulness. If you ever find yourself this happy, note it and remember. Everyone should find a way to live at least part of their life this way.

After serious internal deliberation, I championed the upgrade to PHP5.1, to which we were the first large site to migrate. We may have been the most heavily trafficked PHP site at the time. We upgraded right after the first official release and worked to fix performance problems with the core APC team.[41] Facebook was like that. We were afraid of nothing, as we brought in the best technology and hired the best people, for we knew we could find the brains to fix anything that went wrong.

---

41 Alternate PHP Cache. The standard, not the alternate, way of making PHP applications scale and run fast.

I've found something to put here. Now it's <u>your turn</u>.

Hiring was a perpetual challenge. Before I arrived a mostly
symbolic recruiting tactic involved parking a huge wooden
Italian chef outside of the office door, and while usually he
was expected to hold some restaurant's pizza menu, he
showcased our current open positions, with VP of engineering
at the top. I was involved in most engineering hires at this
time, and while my main concern was whether the candidate
could do an excellent job on the set of projects I knew were
coming up, Zuck, Scott, and others wanted simply brilliant
geniuses who could learn to do whatever we needed, now or in
the future. It takes longer to find geniuses, but I must say,
with its ability to draw on the pool of 8 million college student
users, eventually the company succeeded. While I suppose
subconsciously I was looking for more engineers like myself,
the company explicitly and correctly decided that Scott was
the proper model engineer.

Like Google, Facebook wanted super smart engineers who
could own a project and deliver amazing technology. Unlike
Google, however, Facebook gave more weight to sheer
intellectual brilliance than experience or a demonstrated
ability to deliver a great product. This tends to select for
younger engineers. Also Google tends to hire known experts
in specific areas, while Facebook encouraged engineers to be
generalists.[42] Nevertheless, even with our reputation and

---

42 Well, Google also hires brilliant generalists. Google hires anyone
brilliant. I've heard of a secret plan to build an underground tunnel from
the site of the Stanford graduation ceremony to the Googleplex.

Go do. Build your idea. Share for help.

ability to pay top dollar in the heart of Silicon Valley, it still took tremendous time, effort, and dedicated recruiters to build out the team.

One hiring story showcases Zuck's tremendous integrity. Randi,[43] his sister, now works at Facebook, and her interview happened right next to me, since that was where two open chairs sat on one of those very late work nights. He gave her nothing that everyone else didn't have, and insisted on her earning a strictly market-based salary, repeating that nepotism was something he wouldn't accept. My easy role was convincing her that he was being fair and not just playing out some childhood revenge fantasy.

The engineering culture evolved away from having any architects or managers because all of the engineers were brilliant, motivated, and sharp enough on all the product details to not need formal management. Much later, as I approached my one year anniversary departure from Facebook, I started feeling Old.[44] But only in relative terms, since everyone around me was so young, inspired, and brilliant. In absolute terms, I only felt that way when I started getting sleepy around midnight, and if my back hurt after sleeping on the couch.

---

43 http://harvard.facebook.com/profile.php?id=4617

44 Whenever I feel Old I run a marathon. It's worked for me so far.

I've found something to put here. Now it's your turn.

That's how I started at Facebook. While it was a genuine Silicon Valley early startup experience, an even earlier story needs to be told. I arrived on the scene when Facebook was already a big deal for college students, and when there was plenty of cash to have an office and hire a full engineering team. But, as you know, Facebook started in a Harvard dorm room, on one server with no cash and few expectations of greatness.

Facebook's Beginning

The elite hacker stalks briskly through the cold evening air. Cradling a laptop, he slips through the closing door into yet another Harvard dorm building. He's determined to overcome the IP-based security scheme that limits access to students' personal information to the residents of the dorm in which they live.[45] Blocking the flow of information is wrong, instinct and the most powerful conviction scream within him.

Scanning the walls, he sees his objective—an Ethernet port that uses the address inside this dorm. He plugs in and quickly grabs the pictures and profiles of all the residents. Then he moves on to his next target. By day's end, he's ripped into his laptop enough information to build interesting profiles for everyone at Harvard, a Mark Zuckerberg Production, a gift to the Harvard community.

In late October 2003, Facemash.com lit up Harvard. Pictures of two randomly selected Harvard students would appear for a basic Hot-or-Not comparison. The site lasted only a day or so, but pulled down 22,000 hits from 450 people. Already the

---

45 This only means that everyone within a given dorm has access to information on only the residents of that dorm, and that you can only access that info from that IP address. Zuck still laughs at the idea that he was some hardcore hacker, as the school administration tried to label him. They just had a lame security model.

I've found something to put here. Now it's your turn.

seeds of Facebook were planted.[46] Some Harvard student
groups were not amused, however. Zuck took the site down
and apologized,[47] saying he hadn't intended to hurt people's
feelings. "I'm not willing to risk insulting anyone. . . . I'm a
programmer and I'm interested in the algorithms and math
behind [the Web site]".

The Harvard administration specified what privacy rules were
unacceptable, and, by demonstrating that a site like Facebook
could overcome those complaints, he managed to create a site
private and safe enough that students could trust it. Over
several days, he coded the initial version of Facebook.com,
powered by a beverage-not-to-be-named[48] and probably plenty
of happy adrenaline.

The Web site, originally named thefacebook, was initially
released on February 4, 2004. Each entry included a picture, a
list of personal attributes on the right, and a list of friends.
Notably, the item of greatest interest to his college audience—
sex—was front and center. The attributes "looking for" and
"relationship status" showed what kind of relationship might
be available with the person in question, and "interested in"

---

46 http://www.thecrimson.com/article.aspx?ref=349808

47 For what? For dissing the people who were scored as ugly, for
appearing insensitive, for putting the whole thing behind him so he
could build another similar site.

48 Not coffee. Don't even think about bringing that brew into the same
room as Zuck.

Go do. Build your idea. Share for help.

confirmed that it could be with you. An early Easter egg enabled someone to message "sex?" from a mobile phone and if yes, the reply would be the partner's room number. Pretty hot stuff.

And it worked. Within the first three weeks, more than 6,000 Harvard students had joined. An early Wayback Machine page from February 12, 2004, shows the original front page, Harvard only.[49]

Facemash.com was repurposed around this time to show an individual's "Buddy Zoo," foreshadowing some of what Facebook would become. In the actual words of the site on February 6, 2004, here's how it worked:

> Users submit their AIM Buddy Lists to the site. Then, BuddyZoo runs all kinds of analysis on the data, letting you:
>
> * Find out which buddies you have in common with your friends.
> * Measure how popular you are.
> * Detect cliques you're part of.
> * See a visualization of your Buddy List.
> * View your Prestige, computed the way Google computes PageRank to rank web pages.

---

49 Facebook.com doesn't have good coverage on the Wayback Machine, and MySpace blocks all (well-behaved) crawlers so it has no coverage at all. You can see how the site looked back until March 2005 under thefacebook.com's entries.(See http://web.archive.org/web/20040212031928/http://www.thefacebook.com/)

I've found something to put here. Now it's your turn.

> * See the degrees of separation between different
> screennames.
> * More features are still on the way. Check back in
> a few days. "

It was already clear that Facebook was going to be big, since it had exploded across every Ivy League school it had been introduced to and had gathered up to 2 million members. Zuck wanted investment and connections, so during the summer of 2004, Zuck and Dustin made the trek out West. With its concentration of premier educational institutions, like Stanford and Berkeley, and tech companies, like IBM, Cisco, Apple, Yahoo, and Google, Silicon Valley [50] was where everything hot on the Internet was happening.

At the time, Facebook was running on Zuck's personal savings, which he'd accumulated doing various computer related jobs since before high school.[51] Just as it was becoming uncertain how the bandwidth bill would be covered, Peter Thiel stepped in. Founder of PayPal, early investor in LinkedIn, and fierce Libertarian, Thiel made a saving angel

---

50 My childhood home. Three cheers for hometown pride! Yes, I know that the Valley has more and more offshore competition, and that many other tech hubs exist in America (http://paulgraham.com/america.html), and that centralization is decreasingly necessary. Personally, I like Oregon.

51 Eduardo Saverin, a wealthy Brazilian student friend, put in a significant amount of capital. He was soon removed, however, perhaps for not contributing in a working capacity, as well as possibly for using the site traffic for his own side business. Startups can have all kinds of convulsions in their early stages.

Go do. Build your idea. Share for help.

investment, which he has said was the best investment at current valuations he had ever made. Perhaps he felt that way because once, on his birthday, the Facebook leaders arranged for him to receive hundreds of pokes and messages from beautiful girls.

So, how did Zuck and Sean get together, since their meeting was so important to the future of Facebook? Which brilliantly networked headhunter set that up? In what fancy restaurant did they first sketch their plans on a fine napkin and toast their success? Indeed, they had made actual plans once or twice to meet, back in Boston, I think, but those somehow fell through.

In actuality, Sean met Zuck completely by chance on the street in front of the rented house he was sharing in Palo Alto. Since Sean had no clear place to stay at the time, Zuck let him crash at the house. As they talked their plan emerged. That management recruiting technique was never to be repeated, but maybe it's why Zuck and Sean could think that a wooden chef outside their office door might bring in a VP of Engineering.

Additional rounds of funding totaling over $35 million from Accel, Greylock, and Meritech Capital ensured that Facebook had sufficient cash for any existing plans and contingencies, and, since Facebook was clearly successful and more or less profitable, it was in the driver's seat during all financing negotiations. VCs usually demand special protection for their capital, and often the companies they invest in experience heavy dilution. But not when multiple VCs are competing to get in on the deal. The very evening that Zuck closed the initial funding round of $11 million (he may even have had the check on him as he went to some fast food joint in East Palo Alto) he was held up at gun point. The most exhilarating and the most terrifying moments of his life happened within hours of each other.

One important money saving characteristic at Facebook, is that the leadership team has always known when to pull the plug on efforts that don't fit the vision and to prune employees to ensure the best allocation of resources. Even when someone was a good worker, I've seen management try out a replacement to see if see if he or she would be a better fit. While Noah and I could be seen as personal casualties of this policy, in reality it is best for both the employees and the company, as long as it affects so few people that the ones that remain don't feel in personal risk themselves, or have just enough concern that it hones their focus and productivity.

In one all-hands meeting, I recall Zuck saying that anything less than full commitment saps the focus and strength of the other employees. Plenty of misunderstandings may have occurred that have led to excellent, dedicated people being let off the train, but to avoid letting anyone go would be bad policy. A successful company should stand firmly against allowing people to just holding on for the ride. A company's vision is only as strong as the shared vision of its employees, and any voices that don't resonate[52] with the leaders' vision weaken the company.

Some companies lack vision. Even while the executives parade out one vision after another, the employees go about their day without thinking about it or understanding it. Such companies need visionary thinkers, creative minds, *and* need to liberate those minds to do their magic, or inevitably the company will not benefit[53] and possibly those minds will be lost.[54]

Facebook, on the other hand, has a very clear, powerful vision, and since most employees come at it from the same place—college—it comes as naturally as breathing air to them. Now that the site is open to everyone, Facebook would benefit from more employee diversity, in order to continue channeling their target audiences.

Few hugely successful sites are created by a single technologist who handles both product and engineering. Zuck is one of those rare talents who can do both, and he succeeded because he chose a manageable problem right at the center of his experience and competency. He knew what he could do and also understood his own limitations well enough to find the right people to cover for him in those

---

52 http://en.wikipedia.org/wiki/Tacoma_Narrows_Bridge#Collapse

53 http://en.wikipedia.org/wiki/Xerox_PARC

54 http://www.anvari.org/shortjoke/Funny5/3421.html

I've found something to put here. Now it's your turn.

areas. No one can do everything, or even be really good at
many things, so Zuck's talent was in pushing himself to his
full ability on a small but important problem. Or more
accurately, as if there were about five or ten of himselves. He
had too much to do, but he was able to fully understand all
aspects of what his project and know what he needed to do
every step of the way, right up to the point where he was
objectively successful.

Zuck is also good at recognizing what he doesn't know and
finding the right person to teach him. He wastes no time with
fools, and can drill straight to the point so fast it can hurt.
Nevertheless, he listens well and is always learning. Zuck also
keeps things simple. When he makes a presentation at an all-
hands meeting, he usually has no more than two to five simple
slides, most with only a single bullet point (i.e., Company
goal: Grow site usage) or a two-color pie chart (i.e., Something
I can't tell you about MySpace). This really helps with the
uniform, understandable-vision thing. On the other hand, I
don't know how many diverse opinions Zuck hears, and I don't
know how many in the company get to talk with him regularly.
I don't think he had any takers when he introduced CEO office
hours.

Google is notoriously engineer-driven, and the business plan
came late because the VCs were comfortable funding the
people behind the technology. Those people were able to
build an excellent search engine and grow their leadership

Go do. Build your idea. Share for help.

skills even faster than they grew their company. Pierre Omidyar, eBay's creator, built the first generation technology himself, but was quick to partner with MBA-holding friends to run the business side of the company. He continued to phase himself out whenever he found people who did what he did as well as he could. Finally, he was just the soul of the company, ensuring that it was consistent with his values and core vision.

The Google founders acknowledged some limitations by hiring Eric Schmidt as an experienced CEO to be the prominent adult in the room, but they still maintain a two-to-one majority in their unique executive triumvirate. Noam Wasserman conducted extensive research and concluded that startup founders end up either as kings or rich[55] but rarely both. He noted that Gates and Dell are famous exceptions, figures that Zuckerberg perhaps aims to emulate.

Whatever he actually said in public, YouTube founder Steve Chen was clearly interested in being acquired. His intent was clear. Gates, Ellison, Larry, and Sergey were also clear. Zuck has said, both publicly and privately, that he's not looking to be acquired, and certainly his behavior is consistent with his words. His is a very bold position.

---

55 http://founderresearch.blogspot.com/2005/11/rich-versus-king-core-concept.html

---

I've found something to put here. Now it's your turn.

Even having a clear vision and knowing everything about how to build it still doesn't guarantee a successful company. Let's talk in more detail about who contributed to the Facebook product and how it happened.

The Team and What We Made

Ezra[56] was Product. That is why he can't send himself off to law school. From well before the time I started, Ezra was making important product decisions and coordinating whatever was happening on the site. Ezra had no product management experience before coming to Facebook. He was contacted while backpacking Europe because Sean Parker had been randomly sleeping at his house during the school year. He started working the day he got back to the States.

Then Noah and Ezra alone were Product. And there were a lot of products, so I can't really tell you how they manage so well. The critical factor in all of Ezra's decisions was that Zuck needed to agree with them and that none of them made the engineers go truly ape-shit. Most of Noah's and Ezra's time seemed to be spent talking through the page layout with the designers, answering engineers emails about whether to do something this way or that, and entering hundreds of pre-release bugs. Having designers[57] meant that Zuck had eight hands. Aaron was Zuck's first designer and he created new fonts and wrote Mac desktop software on the side. Aaron

---

56 http://www.facebook.com/profile.php?id=202801

57 Bryan, Sol, and others. Bryan worked somewhere around ninety-six hours his first week doing Facelift. Sol stands as he works, which just looks as cool as his salutation ("take it light") sounds, though he says it just keeps him awake.

I've found something to put here. Now it's your turn.

taught the organization that designers should be very technical. I'm not sure if Aaron was full time at Facebook or at UC Berkeley or both, but he was the one person whom I was sure that I never knew where he was. When he's focused, he's the most productive front-end guy I've seen. But even The Man was sometimes stymied generating that focus.

Nico, who is old like me, was one of my best engineer friends.[58] He runs marathons and is an accomplished drummer. Nico kept me sane, as nothing ever pulls him out of his rhythm. Chris Cox is also a musician and a philosopher with deep spiritual interests. In general, these geniuses, like the other engineers at Facebook, were talented in many ways, and it was fun to just watch them. My only talent was throwing empty bottles into the recycling container from across the room, but fear of injuring the graffiti forced me into semi-retirement.

I got to know two other members of my team quite well. Jordan[59] was a sophomore at Stanford and he was the brightest kid ever knew. He'd look right to the hardest part of any project and dash out possible solutions like an idea machine. It always took longer for him to explain his solution to me than it took for me to explain the project or task. One challenge with hiring geniuses, though, is that they want to do

---

58 In the Real, as well as the Facebook context.

59 http://stanford.facebook.com/profile.php?id=207427

Go do. Build your idea. Share for help.

things cleverly while challenging themselves to learn all kinds of stuff around it at the same time. Whether the product is ever finished, or whether it actually does anything useful, is sometimes secondary to whether it was a fun and challenging process. On the other hand, he can get impressive things done, as he did as a senior intern by building a full administrative Web application for his high school, which I think is used by all the teachers and students even now.

In many ways his diametric opposite was <u>Christopher</u>,[60] the prototypical effective <u>consultant/contractor</u>.[61] He'd finish a task in the simplest, least complex way possible, ideally mapping it to some code he'd written before or found. Chris was customer focused. He has built out a successful business by himself, demonstrating that an individual with a balance of people and technical skills can be independent.

Steve Grimm was another key consultant. Even after the company decided to continue exclusively with full-time employees, Steven (and Jordan) made the cut. They were just too brilliant to let go. Steve would be put on whatever distinct piece of the application that was most difficult, and he would attack it meticulously. Steve visited China where he noticed the entertaining fact that the covers of pirated DVDs were often printed with completely random movie reviews—

---

60 <u>http://www.facebook.com/profile.php?id=31601658</u>

61 <u>http://softwebstudios.com</u>

I've found something to put here. Now it's <u>your turn</u>.

including some that noted that the movie contained within
was simply awful.

Every startup has too much work for too few people. Amy was
the principle database engineer, which meant that she did
every single bit of database-related work for over 200 servers.
I enjoyed running my all-night schema-conversion scripts with
her for three consecutive nights. Night work is purely a joy for
the young who don't have to take their kids to school at 8:30
the next morning.

Jeff Rothschild, in his various incarnations of VP of
Engineering, was the most critical hire in the history of
Facebook. He made many of the right calls on hiring and
technology, and kept the ship stable until TS came aboard. Jeff
was so important that Zuck offered to create a nickname for
him, to bind him closer to the company. Unfortunately, the JRo
nickname didn't stick, despite the fact that JRo is the hippest
VP of Engineering ever. Seriously! In his spare time he fixed
most serious hardware problems before the vendors could
even figure out what was going on. He intimidated vendor
sales staffs by telling them, "No, I actually have built that kind
of product myself, and that's not how it works."

Matt Cohler[62] wore the most hats. He was VP of whatever
needs doing most today—perhaps the most important VP at
any startup. Matt is incredibly thoughtful and kind when he's

---

62 http://www.facebook.com/profile.php?id=304760

Go do. Build your idea. Share for help.

not distracted: He actually sent my daughter (sculptor of this ferocious girly dinosaur[63]) a lava lamp that he'd seen her oohing and aahing over one time when she came to visit, on my self-designated bring-the-kids-to-work-day. He's also always typing on his Crackberry, and we rescheduled a lunch meeting 7 times over 2 months.

Matt at one time also led the charge on behalf of Pokey (recall the fine artwork of the hedgehog from the introduction), who could have been the unforgettable symbol of a major product direction, before real marketers were hired and shut him down. Pokey represents poking, an original Facebook activity. Pokey's last name is Schlegel[64], since that may be Matt's favorite German philosopher. At one time, people actually seriously did spend hours discussing the details of Pokey.

Matt's counterweight was the COO, Owen,[65] who was responsible for translating the vision into a massive written plan and then glaring at people with his steely eyes until they ran away to make it happen. Owen's other claim to fame was his resemblance to Steve Carroll from the movie *The 40 Year Old Virgin*. Of all people at Facebook, Owen was the most distraught about my departure, I think because it left him as the only person at the company with a little daughter, who, on

---

63 http://www.facebook.com/album.php?aid=2000674&id=19401714
64 http://www.encyclopedia.com/html/S/SchlegelF.asp
65 http://www.facebook.com/profile.php?id=6712782

I've found something to put here. Now it's your turn.

one of her visits, told me what her Daddy really does: He
doesn't do *anything*; he just talks all the time.

TS was hired in the Fall of 2005 to be VP of Product
Engineering, I think. As far as I could tell, every engineer
reported directly to him so he was very important and very
busy. He started the Yahoo Messenger group, and made it
successful. Universally he was called TS because few could
remember "Ramakrishnan." His first name is even longer. He
said he likes his real first name, though, as he spewed it just
once during his introduction, and will keep it since his parents
went through *so* much trouble creating it for him. At Facebook
I reported to Zuck and TS, all the while doing most of my work
for Dustin. (Well, mostly I reported to Trac,[66] which, once I put
in the notification feature, politely thanked me and everyone
else for doing such nice work for it.)

Kent Schoen was one of the engineering types who actually
interviewed at the Facebook before I did. He was scared away
by the graffiti the first time, though.[67] I lobbied him daily. He
was shy and played hard-to-get, but he joined during the
summer and soon became responsible for all of the
advertising technology. Kent was unique in that he was a good

---

66 The bug tracking system . . . considering the supremely informal
reporting structure.

67 Actually, no one was there to talk to him except Matt. The odd thing
about that is that Matt was there. A main reason Susie was hired was so
that we'd get organized enough to stop standing up important interview
candidates.

Go do. Build your idea. Share for help.

programmer, an even better technical architect, and yet he was someone you'd like to hang out with. He's a genuine people person. He's even outgrown his habit of calling everyone outside his immediate vicinity "those clowns."

Kent was unusual in that he liked building advertising technology to, you know, make money for the company. Zuck only liked money that came from advertising, and he didn't even like *that* very much. I think he had to have been physically tied up at some executive meeting to accept the ad on the left side of the page. Again, Zuck was right in not copying the MySpace model of putting ads everywhere, which used to have more. Popups, even!

Facebook has much more traffic and inventory than it can sell. Facebook now serves many billions of pageviews a month. If it just sold cheap crappy ad network CPM ads (at, like, $1-$3 CPM[68]) across all of its inventory, it could earn tens of millions of dollars every month. But they would just annoy people, and Zuck *loves* his users. Ow! Zuck just mentally hit me! I meant to say "his student community on the site."

---

68 Possibly, MySpace can only get 10 cents(http://www.techdirt.com/articles/20060424/0749243.shtml). That's not the only thing wrong with it. I don't know Facebook's real CPM (http://www.micropersuasion.com/2006/05/correction_comi.html), and if I did they'd have to shoot me.

I've found something to put here. Now it's your turn.

Kent likes to be creative so they are a good match, whenever
Zuck, TS, or a product person stops for even a second to think
about ads, that is.

Shoot. All of this reminiscing reminds me that I never sent a
"bye" email when I left. Well, here goes: "At least I know we'll
always know how to stay in touch. Thanks for reminding me
what it was like to be young and in love." If you are expecting
a holiday card from me, know that they come in the Spring.

How did we all work together? Not in meetings, which were
rare and often spontaneous. This is in line with industry
trends.[69] I liked meetings more than other folks because I
wanted more architecture and planned collaboration. Everyone
else seemed to prefer autonomy and quick code iterations.
Code reviews were required off and on, and whenever they
were done, were worth their weight in gold.[70]

Facebook Photos is the best model for demonstrating how
major applications were built:

---

69 "Meetings are Toxic", Getting Real, (http://getreal.37signals.com).

70 Nobody ever prints anything, remember. But they were still precious,
since this was the only opportunity, aside from bug fixing, to look at
anyone else's code. However, quick iterations on one's own code,
ambitious deadlines, and heavy scope creep (since real specs were
almost never made), meant little time for reviews or design. In Japan
there was little urban planning so the streets look like the random
cracks in pottery, whereas Paris or newer American cities have a solid
grid framework. Facebook's code architecture certainly tends toward the
organic growth end of that spectrum.

Go do. Build your idea. Share for help.

1. Find a genius engineer who will forego eating and sleeping for two months.

2. Give him the vision.

3. Give him a designer, so that a) he doesn't need to think about how the pages look and instead can focus on function, and b) he immediately knows what the pages will be and how they will work.

4. Get out of the way. Talking to you could make him sleepy or hungry.

5. When it is done, bless it and say it is exactly what you wanted.

The three key points to remember are:

1. Don't change your vision.

2. Make sure he's a genius before starting, by testing him on smaller projects.

3. Ensure that the designer stays ahead of the functionality, since this is the engineer's umbilical cord to reality.

By the way, genius engineers are rare. Obviously, don't limit your talent pool with sexism, racism, nationalism, or doesn't-match-my-expectations-ism. At Facebook, all the early engineers were white men in their early twenties, so I used the pronoun "he." My daughter wants to be a scientist (or an an artist, today), and <u>Ruchi</u>[71] is just one example of an exceptional female engineer.

Photos also had very effective "pro<u>doug</u>" management,[72] which ensured that the features where clearly defined and worked with everything else that was happening around the company.

I experienced one "employee awards" ceremony. I only won the "most likely to sleep under his desk overnight" prize, sharing it with Nick Heyman. A photograph of us doing just that during one of our work marathons was shown during the ceremony. Noah picked up the prestigious "most likely to invite someone for lunch" award. His photo was graced with a smiling picture of the man with the caption, "Hey, I don't know you, but did you know that Facebook has a free lunch? You should come check it out." Noah earned this by leading a parade of the best looking[73] girls seen in the building.

Ears and Spirit of the Company

Facebook's customer service team is huge, with over twenty people. It has always been that way, since Zuck understood

---

71 <u>http://www.facebook.com/profile.php?id=4801660</u>

72 <u>http://www.facebook.com/profile.php?id=1707516</u>

73 Best looking, right after his girlfriend (http://www.facebook.com/profile.php?id=2531387), of course. Hey, his girl has the bod of a marathoner.

---

the importance of communicating with his audience. What's more, they got to sit at the nice desks, better than or equal to everyone else.

At some large corporations, customer service is a high-turnover, low-status job. Some companies farm it out to call centers in India or rural Utah where computer generated metrics require reps to churn through a certain number of calls/email per hour, sometimes with scheduled bathroom breaks. Some kids hope that customer service jobs are a foot in the door at a big company, but outsourcing has largely closed that door, if it ever was a real career path at a single company.

When treated well, though, customer service folks are some of the best problem solvers in a company. Even better, these folks have decided that they want to be cheerful during their workday.

At Facebook, customer service embodies the student user. Literally. Customer service was mostly made up of heavy Facebook users from Stanford. Customer service often knew exactly what student users wanted, and could communicate that clearly to the heavy Facebook-using student engineers who would immediately make the change. Everyone was a user. On one of my first days I asked Dustin what his IM address was, and he answered "There's this Web site where you can look that up. It's called Facebook." How useful it is to

I've found something to put here. Now it's <u>your turn</u>.

have a large pool of smart, prototypical users right there next to you.

And they were nice and fun to talk to! Not like all the boring engineers I'd sit with the rest of the time. The funniest regular meeting presentation I ever saw was by CS team lead Paul Janzer. It won his entire group a relocation up to the nicer, sunnier third floor.

The following are samples of actual user questions, reproduced here as best as possible from memory:[74]

- I'm looking for a girl named Cathy in Chicago. Could you please tell me where I can find her, because I'd like to see her again.

- My college can't even provide me an education, much less an email address. Let us on the damn site!

- How can I find my own profile?

- I think my [boyfriend or girlfriend] is cheating on me. Let me into their account so I can find out.

- (from a high school student) . . . so please help me with that as you can. because i want to look cool like my friends. at least i hope they'll think I'm cool.

---

74 I can't remember what I had for lunch. I wish I'd taken notes about important items like these.

Go do. Build your idea. Share for help.

The current director of customer service, Tom LeNoble, is a calm, capable, and organized guy. He replaced me as the ranking member of the age diversity program. He's also the only person who ever asked me for a printout of anything.[75]

The Competition

Facebook wasn't always the guaranteed winner in the college space. ConnectU and a bunch of alumni sites like reunion.com preceded Facebook, and other competitors have followed.

Around October 2005, XuQa shot into existence, and into supergrowth prominence, by basically unethically crawling thousands of Facebook pages and emailing bogus invitations to join. Facebook responded by setting XuQa as a "porn word" and blocking the piracy, after which XuQa's site traffic died back a bit and then mostly flat-lined at around half a million members. Still, it looks like XuQa has achieved the critical mass that will allow it to survive for a while. It has

---

75 I, on the other hand, killed more trees than the rest of the engineers combined. It seems like only engineers older than thirty print stuff. One management strategy I used while leading a five-to-nine-person major product push involved printing out all of the significant user-facing screens, putting them up on a wall, and having everyone scribble on them. On the positive side, we actually did get feedback, and everyone in the company could viscerally feel the rate of progress. Unfortunately, it was physically tied to a wall, and was hard to version and change. It finally ended up as a large paper salad under my desk after the office move. I also helped initiate the use of Trac (http://trac.edgewall.org/), which is still in wide internal use, along with Basecamp (http://basecamphq.com).

I've found something to put here. Now it's your turn.

differentiated itself by offering some unique characteristics, such as using peanuts as a currency, kisses, secret crushes, etc., and by having a crisper, flashier user interface. It was able to build the site in one summer by hiring at least twenty Pakistani engineers. Its engineering is still based out of Karachi. Just recently, XuQa has differentiated itself more strongly by turning itself into a game, making the acquisition and use of peanuts into a core purpose of the site[76].

Bebo.com claims huge membership and usage numbers, numbers the company has been unwilling to confirm or explain to me. Alexa still shows the site as in the low end of the U.S. top 500, though growing fast.

Many, many other social sites are pure vaporware, or are not differentiated enough to overcome the first-mover challenge. While MySpace and Facebook have a first-mover advantage with strong network effects, plenty of opportunity exists for supplementing the leaders in specific niches, or even surpassing them with a superior offering.

Latecomers without a significant sponsor to pay indefinite losses may need to make ethical compromises, sometimes against their larger competitors, but also against their own users. I can't believe that XuQa's full profiles are open to

---

76 First rule of marketing: If you can't be first or second in your category, make a new category in which you are first. See http://software.gigaom.com/2006/08/15/xuqa-its-all-a-game/.

Go do. Build your idea. Share for help.

Google and anyone else in the world. However, even the market leader doesn't appear to be particularly concerned about privacy: MySpace shuts out obedient crawlers, but bad crawlers can result in your picture (and full profile, unless you are diligent with your privacy settings) ending up on http:// myspacehotties.net/. This would be construed as good almost only if you are a porn star, most of whom have flocked to MySpace. The site also leaves all information fully open to any member. I can search for anyone and see their everything just by registering a meaningless account.

Do these companies do this because their users are clueless and/or truly unconcerned about their privacy? Relative to these sites, Facebook is good about privacy, by limiting profile view to friends and the users own networks and by adding some field-specific privacy controls. Nevertheless, only a very small minority of users modify their default privacy settings.

Making Money

How does Facebook make money? Easily. Any way it wants. Ooooh, you bought this book to get some real insights. Gotcha!

First, let me tell you how this book is going to make me some money. (Hint: in the same way that Facebook makes money.) On the Web site associated with this book, I'm going to sell some ads. If you happen to own or manage a major brand,

I've found something to put here. Now it's your turn.

and you want your brand permanently associated with the glory of Facebook, in black and white on beautiful recycled paper no less, just send me a check.[77] Every word here is God's honest truth,[78] except where it's dripping with sarcasm or, worse yet, humor.

If only we, our own lowly and humble selves at fbbook.com, had the market visibility, relationships, and cream-of-the-Internet-crop sales team that Facebook has to reach potential marketers. I also wish we had complete penetration of the college demographic. While this wasn't true a year ago, I suspect that Facebook now quite easily commands the interest of anyone with a product targeting the college-age population, without even trying that hard.

Facebook makes money in two ways: ads on the site with super-fancy targeting (based on the information users enter into the site about themselves) and sponsored groups, events, and notifications.

---

77 Given global warming (climatecrisis.net) and peak oil (lifeaftertheoilcrash.net), I think I'll not buy Japan (http:// realestate.theemiratesnetwork.com/developments/dubai/ world_islands.php) for a cool $7 million.

78 Sometimes I have paid affiliate links, which are still rare in books. Dunno why.

Go do. Build your idea. Share for help.

In the summer of 2005, I enjoyed a lunch with Apple's <u>Dave
Morin</u>[79] and Matt. We discussed the natural fit between the
Facebook and the Apple brands. Dave architected the first big
marketing deal on Facebook by creating the Apple Students
Group. The group was created around the idea that college
students love cool, <u>well-designed</u> technology, <u>especially when
it's related to music,</u>[80] and Facebook would be a great place to
hold a worthwhile conversation. I was there at the initial chat
about whether Apple could co-brand a store on the site, or co-
market iTunes. The <u>group now has a half-million members,</u>[81]
and iTunes has given away almost 250 million free songs to
students.

I bet the Apple and Facebook relationship will continue to
strengthen over time, despite Facebook's <u>massive advertising
deal with Microsoft,</u>[82] both for sponsored listings and
contextual ads.

---

79 <u>http://www.facebook.com/profile.php?id=10200882</u>, <u>http://
davemorin.com</u>

80 <u>http://www.amazon.com/exec/obidos/ASIN/B000HXV36K/
ptradescom-20</u>, <u>http://www.amazon.com/exec/obidos/ASIN/
B000BNLGJA/ptradescom-20?
creative=327641&camp=14573&adid=1XFD7TG89WX1VRCNNZWR&link_
code=as1</u>

81 <u>http://www.facebook.com/group.php?gid=2204894392</u>

82 <u>http://www.techcrunch.com/2006/08/23/facebook-does-ad-deal-
but-not-with-google/</u>

I've found something to put here. Now it's <u>your turn</u>.

A third way Facebook makes money is with Flyers. This
method is the most fascinating to me because it's a Facebook
feature that just happens to bring in money, by allowing user
advertising on their own network. If Flyers were free they
would be actually less useful, because limiting postings to
paid advertisements reduces clutter and spam. Facebook
Flyers are superior in every way to the archaic method of
posting leaflets around campus.

So, Facebook makes money in three ways: sponsored groups,
targeted ads, and flyers.

What if a social network company wanted to make a lot of
money?

Lets consider this from two perspectives: that of a company
with good intentions, and that of an evil company just out to
make gobs of cash, with the inevitable slippery slope between
them.

Many innocuous methods exist for ad or brand placements on
a social network site. If I list Oreo cookies as one of my profile
interests, this could display with a ™ symbol linking to
Nabisco's site, and the Oreo link click-thru to everyone
interested in Oreo's could have Nabisco's and competitors'
paid links at the top. Or Oreo could even be in Nabisco's
preferred font. Or, if I say I like Macs, that statement could be
replaced by the Apple logo. This might look annoying, or look
like we were selling our to our corporate masters, but if we

look only at the words, at the content, the actual information and location doesn't change. People clearly come to Facebook to look at content, not to click on ads, so blending the content with the ads could be very compelling.

If a closed social network is tied or based to a specific geographic location, then many more opportunities open up.

A site could sell or otherwise offer valuable marketing reports to a wide variety of interested parties, since in the aggregate, social network data embodies information about what memes and products are hot among its members. This aggregated information is valuable to outsiders, and the social network company adds value by collecting, filtering, and analyzing this information.

A site could even sell user content, such as an aggregation or collage of nice photos,[83] but while some user agreements do not prohibit it, I suspect it crosses a line beyond which there would be a user backlash.

A site could partner to sell products to its audience, both by sharing its brand and by offering ad space for products available at its own store.

---

83 http://www.facebook.com/group.php?gid=2204268707. Actually, this url probably got into Google by being linked from another site, which is even hotter (http://fsu.facebook.com/album.php?aid=70103&page=1&l=7920d&id=5226986).

I've found something to put here. Now it's your turn.

In general, social network Web sites have tremendous latent value for two reasons. Both reasons are amazing because all of the value is provided by the community, not by the site or by anything the social network site does.

First, within a social network, users want to demonstrate their status and value to the community and they will pay money for "pro" badges (flickr),[84] for virtual flowers (hotornot),[85] or for other virtual digital goods. These, being completely virtual and unreal, have no tangible value whatsoever. Yet they accrue value from how they are used and viewed within the social network.

Second, the members of a social network have a lot of knowledge and skills that are inherently useful to others in the network and to outsiders willing to pay money for them. If the site empowers users to be useful to each other, such as by providing a product/service recommendation interface, the site can take a cut of the value those users offer each other. The founder of hotornot.com describes his unique and long-lasting dating site: Two strangers meet in a bar, one smiles, showing the other person he thinks she's hot. She smiles back, indicating that the feeling is mutual. But someone is going to have to buy drinks, and the bar takes a cut.[86]

---

84 http://www.flickr.com/

85 http://hotornot.com/

86 Actually, what he said was, "someone will have to buy drinks, and that someone will be me."

Go do. Build your idea. Share for help.

People wonder how social networks could have billions of dollars of value. While I'm not sure how much value a billion dollars should have, whether denominated in gold, oil, Big Macs, McMansions, or green pieces of paper, I do believe social networks have a billion dollars in value relative to other Internet properties. First, Facebook either is profitable or is really close to being so. Social networks are not especially expensive to operate. Engineering costs predominate, and writing social networking Web applications isn't hugely difficult, which is why, when you think about it, there are so many of them. Second, the network effects of social networks (once you are on one with all of your friends, you'd all have to move to another one together to have shared value) and the personal effort invested in entering all of your information and your collected usage history at the site, together create a high barrier to entry for new networks. This is why the market leaders maintain their big leads, are frantic about expanding their market share, and why their competitors target niches to establish themselves. Third, as I've shown above, and as many business people smarter than me will soon show you, the monetization of social networks has only just begun.

YouTube was sold to Google for $1.65 billion, and it wasn't even making money. An identity-rich social network, one that holds all of you, not just your videos, can be sticky for a lifetime. Less than 10 percent of Facebook members ever abandon the site permanently. For its core audience, everything social can be transacted inside. Even a small cut of

---

I've found something to put here. Now it's <u>your turn</u>.

those goods and services can result in a tremendous profit. Members of Second Life[87] spend half-a-million dollars each day on . . . nothing. Facebook currently only sells Flyers—but the potential for in-site commerce between members is immense.

Facebook may print money, with an IPO. I'd like to see one! But see, that's why I'm not running the show! Apparently, I have yet to read Seth Godin's *Small Is The New Big*.[88]

Certainly there are advantages to staying privately owned, such as being able to avoid the complex laws and reporting requirements of public companies. A common reason for going public is to raise cash. Facebook doesn't need that. Another reason is to convert equity into cash. A good reason for not going public, which Google's founders partly mitigated by having a highly irregular IPO with a class of shares with much less control/voting power, is a loss of control over the destiny of the company. Zuck carefully cultivates and maintains his effective control.

While offering equity is like printing money, such money has only theoretical value until it is exchangeable. The other startup exit strategy is to be purchased by either a public or private entity. If the purchaser is public and it's mostly an equity deal, it's like an IPO except that someone else has

---

87 http://secondlife.com/

88 http://sethgodin.com/small, http://www.amazon.com/exec/obidos/ASIN/1591841267/ptradescom-20

Go do. Build your idea. Share for help.

already done the paperwork. No one knows if any such event will happen for Facebook, but I've seen Zuck be very reasonable when listening to advice.

"I'll do X until I get bought by Y"[89] is a common Internet business strategy, with Google, Microsoft, Yahoo, CNET, and a panoply of media companies as suitors. Zuck always intended for Facebook to become a viable, profitable business on its own. This is wise, as it maximizes flexibility. It's lucky he enjoys running it so much.

89 http://en.wikipedia.org/wiki/List_of_snowclones

I've found something to put here. Now it's your turn.

The Power of the Social Internet

Flying at 38,000 feet halfway between Lihue and the Aleutian Islands on a United flight to Nagoya, I feel incredibly grateful for our strength. Hydrocarbons give us around <u>150 energy slaves</u>,[90] which we, the billion or so affluent First-Worlders, have deployed to provide a lifestyle better than medieval kings enjoyed. We also have a financial and industrial system that enables us to hire Third World product-producing slaves at less than a dollar per hour. Open Source software, which is basically shared programming resources, drives so much innovation. Thanks to an infrastructure that enables me to buy a laptop for around a week's pay, we technology workers can make contributions way beyond what an average human being could have achieved only ten years ago.

By myself, I couldn't produce even a single part for this laptop, nor the hardware Internet behind it. Yet here it is, ready for me to write a few lines of code, or a few ideas for a book. And if my writing is good, thousands of people will run with it, moving society this way or that way. If it is not good, oh well, too bad for me; the attention of the people and their collected power will go to some other person, site, or idea.

---

90 <u>http://www.earthtoys.com/emagazine.php?</u>
<u>issue_number=06.08.01&article=slaves</u>

A few Internet companies have revolutionized how we live our daily lives. I don't need to worry where I'm going anymore because I'll just find the route on Google Maps on my Treo. I now have far more free email accounts than I need, and I use these and IM for most of my interactions with people. My daughters are lucky I haven't figured out how to brush their teeth over IM yet. But since I have just learned how to <u>fold my shirts by watching this movie</u>,[91] I'm sure that my Facebook peers will find a way to computerize their child rearing when they get around to it. Look, I'm not saying this is good or bad. I'm just saying that that's the way things are going.

At 21, My CEO Is Living His Dream

I am thirty-four years old and have landed in one of the few situations that makes me feel really, really, *really* old. My daughter Mimoli asks me why I've started growing a few gray hairs. I tell her that it's because of her. I'm the only one among over fifty engineers that has a kid. My baby Elin asks where is her bottle. I ask her why at the age of thirty-four I find myself in a corporate age-diversity program.

My CEO is living his dream. Can I do it, too? Can you?

---

91 http://video.google.com/videoplay?docid=4776825453418327083

Go do. Build your idea. Share for help.

On the Internet, nobody knows you're a dog.[92] If you know
that joke, you *are* old. It's from the *The New Yorker*,[93] from
back when it was an important print publication.[94] *The New
Yorker* also beautifully demonstrates our New Media, since it
has been owned since 1985 by Samuel Irving Newhouse, Jr.,[95]
aka Conde Nast. When Rupert Murdoch's News Corp.
purchased MySpace there was initial user concern about
inappropriate media concentration and talk of a boycott.[96]
That effort hasn't stopped MySpace from becoming the No. 6
American Internet property.[97]

Not only can you be anyone on the Internet, you are free to
achieve anything. A key image hosting service, pongo.com,[98]
which helped kickstart eBay, was thought up and run by one
lady in Sitka, Alaska. In the end, it's not all that surprising that

92 http://www.unc.edu/depts/jomc/academics/dri/idog.html

93 http://www.newyorker.com/

94 http://www.levity.com/seabrook/eustace.html

95 Who currently shares two prominent characteristics with Mr.
Zuckerberg, who is theoretically halfway to being on the list of Forbes
billionaires, where Brin and Page are at No. 26 and No. 27, respectively,
with around $13 billion each. (See http://en.wikipedia.org/w/index.php?
title=Category:Jewish-American_businesspeople&from=Sekulow%2C+Jay
+Alan, http://www.forbes.com/lists/2006/10/Rank_1.html)

96 See http://en.wikipedia.org/wiki/News_Corporation, http://
www.mediachannel.org/ownership/chart.shtml, http://www.cjr.org/
tools/owners/, http://digg.com/tech_news/
Myspace_boycott_has_begun,

97 http://alexa.com/data/details/main?url=myspace.com

98 http://web.archive.org/web/20050218033027/http://pongo.com/,

I've found something to put here. Now it's your turn.

a few twenty year olds can create the strongest social network in human history. With the Internet, anyone can achieve anything.

So what is it that holds us back? Why isn't everyone a Mark Zuckerberg, creating powerful Internet applications in their spare time?

Belief and vision are key to success. Zuck was blessed with an amazing early-adoption rate at his first schools, so it didn't take complex analytics or fuzzy math to project that other schools would behave similarly. Even an outsider like me, or my senior-executive-type friends David or Dion, could judge that this was likely. Zuck could see it, and the rock star-like media interviews reinforced his belief. Also, Zuck was blessed with two early executives who shared his vision. Sean Parker had seen rocket-like success, first as a founder of Napster in his college dorm room, and again as a founder of Plaxo.[99] Matt Cohler had seen it at LinkedIn,[100] as well as from his perch as a VC analyst. For them, phenomenal success was the natural course of business.

I'm challenged to maintain this dream vision. I meditate on it regularly, and I'm certain I'll soon get to a point where I can

99 See http://www.facebook.com/profile.php?id=207996, http://www.plaxo.com/

100 See http://www.facebook.com/profile.php?id=304760, http://linkedin.com

Go do. Build your idea. Share for help.

keep it. Protect it. Nurture it. Feed it. Literally like the flame of
creativity and drive within me. It helps that I've always been a
dreamer, in that I can easily get excited about a powerful idea,
and can think only of it, of how to make it work. Keeping that
dream vision strong all the way to the completion of an idea,
that is what makes greatness.

But I lived through the dotcom collapse six years ago. Even
before the dotcom frenzy, I was at Geoworks, which lost to
Microsoft at least twice before selling its engineering team to
Amazon. Geoworks had excellent engineering. It created a PC
windowing system with a tiny memory footprint well before
Windows came along. It ran amazingly fast on my first
Pentium laptop in 1996, but the company was serially
murdered by business failures. Many dreams foundered on
those rocks.[101]

A quick Geoworks aside. Microsoft has smashed many
companies, including Netscape, Corel, Apple (once), IBM
(piecemeal), and Sun (maybe). Geoworks, however, has the

---

[101] I feel like a serious Silicon Valley oldtimer when I write that I was
nearby at the founding of eBay. About two miles from where Omidyar
was typing the initial perl code for eBay, I was on the same ISP
(best.com) typing perl code for agoodstore.com, which was going to be
a marketplace where the profits from all sales were given to the charity
of the buyer's choice. On Memorial Day 1996, the eBay site and mine
got the same amount of traffic (http://earthsoulscience.com/images/
zero small.gif), according to my own logs and The Perfect Store by
Adam Cohen (http://www.amazon.com/exec/obidos/ASIN/
0316164933/ptradescom-20). This is the origin of my cynicism about
my own business acumen.

I've found something to put here. Now it's your turn.

distinction of being smashed by Microsoft two times in exactly the same way.

In the cartoon on the next page, substitute Bill Gates for Rove, saying "We will go directly to the OEMs,[102] give our software away for cheap or for free, leverage our dominant position in other markets, and persist until you run out of money" and you have how Microsoft beat Geoworks (the donkeys) in both the PC and mobile handset markets about a decade apart.

Unfortunately, Geoworks didn't survive until the next election.

Another way that this comic resonates with this book is that Facebook is one of those rare companies that doesn't benefit much from history or experience. There is no clear "again" in the social networking space. Each new successful social networking entry brings new angles, new features, new strengths. "Making money on the Internet" is a known challenge, as are the technical challenges of scaling PHP/ Apache Web sites and massive storage solutions, so experience with these problems is valuable. But for the overall product and business, Facebook must create everything from scratch.

I loved my early Facebook days so much because Zuck and company were completely oblivious to this cynicism and

102 Original Equipment Manufacturer. Companies that make, market, and sometimes directly sell PCs, e.g., HP, Dell, IBM (well, before it sold its PC business to a Chinese company), and Sony.

Go do. Build your idea. Share for help.

therefore immune to being paralyzed by it. I have some lingering business cynicism shared by many late-nineties dotcom investors and <u>one canine sock puppet</u>.[103] Many Geoworkers cured themselves and went onto greater things,[104] but only by believing that they could succeed, and by seeing

---

103 <u>http://en.wikipedia.org/wiki/Image:Pets.com_sockpuppet.jpg</u>

104 Like David Thatcher, who conspired to commit the securities fraud (http://www.usdoj.gov/usao/can/press/ 2004/2004_01_14_thatcher.html) that took down Critical Path (<u>http:// en.wikipedia.org/wiki/Critical_Path%2C_Inc</u>.). And went on to CommerceOne, only to get shafted by Microsoft once again.

I've found something to put here. Now it's <u>your turn</u>.

an opportunity in the business environment around them, like the lucky folks at the Seattle office who were sold to Amazon.

I leaped to LookSmart, which proceeded to lose the search and portal wars to Yahoo and Google. One fond LookSmart memory is of an executive at an all-hands Q&A session in mid-1999, at an expensive San Francisco hotel ballroom, being asked about purchasing Google. He replied that such a move would highly dilute LookSmart's stock.

I'm eternally grateful that I could bask in the Facebook optimism bath for many months. May you all have a chance to experience something like that! It is heaven for the human spirit. And it really makes folks strive to recreate it. Whether it succeeds in the end doesn't matter, because I believe the memory of this feeling will persist and survive any failure. It is so wonderful, that the memory of it outlives anything that follows. I arrived at both LookSmart and Geoworks too late in the lives of those companies to feel their startup fire.

If there is another dotcom-like shakeout after the Web 2.0 boom, how many current wonder-boys will see dreaming as something you do in your twenties?

For even without those experiences of colossal, dramatic failure, for any good idea there are countless critics and numerous competitors. We must try to stay away from negative, critical people.

Go do. Build your idea. Share for help.

One of them will always be with us, however—our inner voice can spew fear and self doubt if we allow it to, if we don't train it. Are my ideas worth anything? Maybe whatever I'm thinking is already well-known by other people. Maybe my best idea is already being finished by some smarter guy at Google. Why would anyone pay attention to me? Or take time to use what I have built. Everyone is so busy. Even my friends, even my good friends, can't always invest time to look at my ideas, and if they can't, why should I believe anyone else will? Being naive and oblivious to doubt and fear can cover for a while, but reality will just make any such weaknesses even more apparent later.

I don't think Zuck has ever had much self-doubt. Obviously, Zuck wasn't always listened to, and his first few public ideas didn't take off. Zuck isn't naive. Pragmatically, he just tries again with his next idea, and persists tenaciously until he achieves success.

For every success, there are hundreds who have had the same or similar idea who gave up, unable to find or keep the passion to succeed. Each one of them would have faced different challenges in their pursuit of success. Some would have been better prepared in some ways. Others would have had uncommon strengths. Yet others would have found help in certain areas. But the passion that leads to success is a flower that withers when exposed to self-doubt, criticism, and loneliness.

I've found something to put here. Now it's your turn.

An essential emotional fortitude is needed for winning with a startup, and it applies to any creative endeavor.

Many scientists and artists have had rich patrons who commissioned their work, But more inspiring are stories of men and women who pursued an idea, devoting their lives to building something without need of external reward or recognition. Many of these passionate strivers have been lost to history, leaving few traces that have lasted more than a millennium. Even fewer of those have kept any of their original meaning.[105]

Will Bill Gates, Linus Torvalds, or any of our generation of technological heroes be remembered in 300 years? Will Google and Yahoo be superseded like so many other high-tech companies in the last thirty years, including DEC, Compaq, Alta Vista, Atari, Silicon Graphics, etc? How can I create anything really meaningful? What is the average age of the billion dollar companies atop the the Alexa Top 25? It must be less than ten, and why does that feel like a long time? Or are we all really just aiming to win money in the dotcom lottery?

---

105 I wonder what Jesus Christ, Bush's "favorite philosopher" (http://www.informationclearinghouse.info/article1168.htm), would think of Evangelical, Crusading Christians (http://www.commondreams.org/headlines03/1016-01.htm) today, and how he would read The New Testament. The DaVinci Code is a fun read, if you can't get yourself through the Apocryphal Gospels (http://www.ntcanon.org/writings.shtml). By the way, Mary Magdalene was his wife.

Go do. Build your idea. Share for help.

At Facebook, we all believed that we were building a social platform that would really change people's lives, and would continue to be useful for a long time.

Privacy Is Essential, Safety Is Presumed

Privacy is essential to trust, and trust is essential to use. Facebook won in the college space because it enabled college students to interact with their natural college communities, and only with those communities. Each college was isolated and protected from the rest of the Internet, sharing a safe private space. Building on natural, existing communities leverages the inherent feeling of trust among their members.

Not only can you be anyone on the Internet, you can also be no one. On MySpace, I'm K.B. "a naked hippie. No, a sociopathic killer" with interests ranging from yoga and nuclear bombs to farming and the color teal. Tom (founder of MySpace and possessor of 108 million friends as of today) and I happen to have the same picture. (He had it first.) In other words, I am obviously not myself on MySpace. On Facebook, on the other hand, I am about half of one of my real selves.

I've found something to put here. Now it's <u>your turn</u>.

A January 27, 2006, <u>Columbia Spectator Staff Editorial</u>
wrote:[106]

> Right now, anyone with a Columbia e-mail address
> can open an account and access a Columbia
> student's profile. This includes administrators,
> staff, and also alumni, many of whom now work at
> firms that recruit at Columbia.
>
> Facebook is, at its heart, a public forum. The
> "terms of use" and "privacy/security" sections of
> the Web site make clear that by registering users
> are, in effect, publicly releasing all information they
> enter. This is an age of limited privacy, and
> students need to be acutely aware of this. It is
> unfortunate but inevitable that Facebook profiles
> will have to be more like resumes than anything
> else. No one should have to explain to an employer
> why they belong to such groups as "Cocainia" or "I
> Wanna Get High."

As far as I can tell, those statements are all accurate. Unless
someone is furling[107] or otherwise saving your profile
regularly (and that is a big if, since it only takes one furling or
one save-as), you can sweep away anything bad that's on your
profile, if you get to a point in your life that it bothers you.

---

106 http://www.columbiaspectator.com/media/storage/paper865/
news/2006/01/27/Opinion/
Staff.Editorial.Transcript.Or.Facebook-2029015.shtml?
norewrite200608081756&sourcedomain=www.columbiaspectator.com

107 Saving a personal copy with a bookmakring service, like deli.cio.us
or furl.net.

Go do. Build your idea. Share for help.

Facebook also lets you carefully tweak your privacy settings and is alert to abuse.

I've just read Bebo's "Online Safety" pages and had a good laugh at how they pretend to do what they can to keep it safe,[108] by handing out valuable tips like "your online friends are not like your real friends" and "don't tell people where you live." Taking Bebo's reasonable advice would require a complete change in usage patterns.[109]

Kids use MySpace to test out various identities, and to get themselves into trouble whenever they put up some real information. The FBI uses it to catch pedophiles. It's really a soft porn site masquerading as a music site (and I have to admit that some of the chicks are quite hot). Go ahead and check it out for that, but not so much that the FBI starts after you.

Huh? The FBI?

---

108 http://www.blogsafety.com/

109 Bebo says, "Never divulge any personal information that could be used to find or identify you in real life in a public forum. Password protect this information. This information includes your real name, address, telephone number, mobile number, your workplace, health club, or links to Web sites or other profiles that might give this information away. It also includes this kind of information about your friends and family. You may be sharing more information than you intended to by including a pic with something showing in the photo." (See http://bebo.com/SafetyTips.jsp)

I've found something to put here. Now it's your turn.

Yeah, duh. Everyone *can* know who you are on the Internet unless you habitually use an anonymizer service.[110] Your IP address is assigned by someone who can trace it to your account number and your identification information. They are actually required to give that to the government, at least in America, by simple court order. And if the request is made under the Patriot Act, the company where you have your account is not allowed to tell you that they gave your information away, or *even* that they were asked for it. Thank you, my big government friends, for keeping me so safe. Google deserves a real thank you for keeping my faith alive by trying, alone among search engines, to stand up to it, while continuing to create useful features that unfortunately further erode my privacy.[111]

My dad, who grew up behind the Iron Curtain and escaped illegally, feels nostalgic these days. For my younger readers,

---

110 There are dozens of resources in the privacy protection space. Anonimizer.com sells software. FreeProxy.ru, if we can count on Russians to protect our own privacy, has a list of proxies, as well as other information. The Tor network provides intellectual heft, while HideMyAss is instantly useful. Since over 98 percent of Internet users now allow cookies, many Web sites, including Facebook, Yahoo, Google, and my own, require cookies for authentication and other critical services. Anonymizers disallow cookies, which, at this time, limits their usefulness. A proxy that stores cookies anonymously seems like a logical next step. (See http://www.freeproxy.ru/en/free_proxy/cgi-proxy.htm, http://en.wikipedia.org/wiki/Tor_(anonymity_network, http://hidemyass.com)

111 http://www.redherring.com/Article.aspx?a=15669&hed=Google +Desktop+Boycott+Urged

---

Go do. Build your idea. Share for help.

think the "Soviet Union" and "the Communist Menace."
Remember those boogiemen of yesteryear? It's why we did
Vietnam. Kinda like what "terrorism" is these days. Anyway, my
dad was often under surveillance by the secret police. The
advantage in those days, though, was that at least he could
see that he was being followed. Now we should, I guess, just
naturally assume that we are.

The globe has shrunk. I'm typing this on a tatami mat in the
heat of southern Japan during the monsoon season. My truly
delightful MacBookPro is seizing up in the heat and humidity.
I'm in a wood and paper house that predates World War II, yet
NTT (Japan's bureaucratic phone monopoly) would be happy
to come out here and, for no charge whatsoever, run a fiber
optic cable to my house so I could have unlimited Internet
access faster than in my San Francisco Bay Area house for $60
per month. I could be nicely logged into Facebook, with IM
and everything, at speeds faster than in Silicon Valley, from
the southern tip of Japan. But then I'd never get this book
written.

A quick word about Japan and Internet privacy. In Japan, there
is never any doubt that the police will find you. They solve
more than 95 percent of serious crimes, whereas the American
police are lucky to solve half. Yesterday the morning news was
all about the abduction for ransom of a famous rich doctor's
college student daughter. Within half a day, the police had
found her in the maze that is Tokyo and captured her three

I've found something to put here. Now it's your turn.

kidnappers. They were Chinese and I guess they thought they were dealing with the Chinese police. The world's police will likely become more like the Japanese, and democracies will likely pass Patriot Act after Patriot Act to empower them. Social networks, search engines, and other hosted web services greatly enable police and government observation and intrusion into your private life by collecting, and keeping indefinitely, a tremendous amount of information about you.

Aside from public safety, the Japanese do at least two other things very well. They can cover their entire coastline with large cement nuggets that look kind of like jacks (but if you've ever played with jacks, you're too old to be reading this book) and pave the waterway of every river with concrete. Alex Kerr explains that this is because cement companies are politically well connected.[112] In America the oil companies are well connected, so California has a challenge worthy of Sisyphus[113] raising its CAFE standards even to the level of China's,[114] let alone Europe's. The second thing they do well is take care of

---

112 http://www.amazon.com/exec/obidos/ASIN/0864423705/ptradescom-20

113 http://ask.yahoo.com/20020613.html

114 Al Gore's movie and book An Inconvenient Truth do a good job of showing how serious global warming is, and how pitifully little we are doing to promote the easy things we could do to address the problem. Unfortunately, there's too much of Al in it, and he forgot to say how sorry he was for really missing his chance between 1992 and 2002. (See http://www.amazon.com/exec/obidos/ASIN/1594865671/ptradescom-20)

Go do. Build your idea. Share for help.

Japanese people, just like Facebook takes care of your social
life.

Facebook: Your Friend in the Online World

People tend to like whatever takes care of them and Facebook
takes care of its users and its employees. If our government
succeeded so well in taking care of us instead of killing our
soldiers in wars of choice and choosing leaders charged with
hurricane response based on their political contributions,[115]
we might again come to believe the phrase "I'm from the
government and I'm here to help."

Facebook helps its users get what they want in college.
Facebook gives users what they want, which for college
students is information about their friends and schoolmates
for the purpose of . . . well . . . sex. And fun social events . . .
which lead to sex. I was there once, well before Facebook
existed, and I had a great time, though for sure not as great a
time as you. But Facebook has greatly streamlined the
process, so students continue to love it. Yes, I oversimplify.
Nevertheless, Facebook's genius has been in identifying the
core needs of its users.

---

115 The governing ability of our Resident is critiqued, in a highly
unbalanced fashion, in Crashing the Gate by Jerome Armstrong and
Markos Moulitsas Zuniga, which also discusses the power and future of
the Internet in a political context. (See http://www.amazon.com/
Crashing-Gate-Netroots-Grassroots-People-Powered/dp/1931498997)

I've found something to put here. Now it's your turn.

Social networking needs to fulfill a purpose or people will not go to the trouble of using it. In college, Facebook lets you know your peers to a depth and breadth that is otherwise impossible. It turns out that some high school students and college graduates need that too, if not as passionately.

As people get older, we don't have as great a need to find out about the new people around us. We have the friends we need, usually. Actually, we often have more friends than we have the time to properly keep. We need to know what's up and what's new with the friends we have. We need to network for business, so there's LinkedIn. The more user needs Facebook can fulfill, the less competitor sites will be necessary.

Facebook also fulfills the core needs of its employees, or of its engineers, at least. I've long aimed to be a geek, so I sit with the geeks. Engineers want very much to make an impact with their work, to see their work used. College-age engineers see nothing on the Internet as impactful as Facebook, since it has shaped their lives since high school, and they see no reason why it shouldn't continue to be the place online they and their friends spend most of their time. So Facebook allows its engineers to own their projects, to feel like they have finished them, and to reap the rewards of the resulting impact.

If a service is useful, people will give it their loyalty, and give up a lot for it, though less eagerly with countable things like money. With Facebook, users used to put up with bugs, privacy issues, and annoying people in their networks because

Go do. Build your idea. Share for help.

it was useful. With Google Sync (a service that restores my browser if it crashes or I move to another computer) I am willing to tell Google everything that I am looking at. With Google Desktop (in which Google keeps an index of all my personal files on some server) I am willing to show Google everything I have, to let it keep that information, and allow it to use it anyway it likes. Sayonara to the last shreds of my privacy. But hey, it's okay; Google's not evil,[116] and I can't stand it when I lose my work context to a rare browser crash. Remember that not evil part, okay guys. Right? Guys? Hello? Are you still listening, or have you become huge and dominant yet?

In what other ways will Facebook become my online friend? Will it somehow change the world, starting with its political election-focused groups and candidate profiles, as blogs may be changing politics?[117] Will an even deeper or more multifaceted purpose for Facebook appear? Since you'll be shaping the future through the way you use the site, or the way you encourage and build alternatives, what do you think? [118]

LinkedIn is for improving business results. SimplyHired.com and karmaone.com are for getting a job. MySpace is for

116 http://investor.google.com/conduct.html

117 http://www.amazon.com/exec/obidos/ASIN/1931498997/ptradescom-20

118 http://www.fbbook.com/fblog/facebook-future

I've found something to put here. Now it's your turn.

everything and nothing at the same time. Facebook is about interests, so maybe it will become a vehicle for enabling progress on those by structuring your alignment with similar people, as bookmark sharing services like furl or diigo do for information professionals like researchers, librarians, and authors. So many Internet activities are naturally social, some combination of vertical and general social networks (collaborating probably, under some common trust model) will recreate the Internet as a social space.

The Internet and Global Social Networks

There are now more Internet users in China and Japan together than in the United States. If the trend of the last five years continues, there will be twice as many Internet users in China as there are people in the U.S.[119] The web will continue to internationalize, and I'm going to need to learn more Chinese, because the few social networking sites in China don't have any English on them.

Facebook has taken off among UK college students. Multiply.com took a big investment from a Japanese company and is set to launch in Japan. The fast growth of Friendster and Orkut in Asia and Latin America hindered their U.S.-based operations. Orkut is today 8th in the world in reach (3-4% of

---

119 Detailed world Internet usage statistics can be found at http://www.Internetworldstats.com/stats.htm.

Go do. Build your idea. Share for help.

daily internet users) according to Alexa, but in the U.S. market is 39th, between 38. Netflix and 40. CareerBuilder. A Chinese knockoff of Facebook, Xiaonei.com, was launched in 2005, and claims to have reached one million members. It was recently bought out, despite its bad karma: The IP theft was so blatant that it launched with the Facebook stylesheet in its html source. They hadn't even bothered to rename it. Or perhaps it isn't serving the right needs because its rules are different in very interesting ways[120]: you can change your page background and music, you can count and see everyone who has looked at you and see how many hits someone else's profile received, any email address in China works to create an account that can see all profiles.

Even North America is experiencing globalization. Canadian AirG has 10 million exclusively mobile phone-based users,[121] including a million strong Spanish-speaking community, Conexion Latina. Korea's largest mobile phone operator recently launched its Cyworld product[122] in the U.S. market, with clearly global intentions.

Building a basic social networking site is not that hard: Zuck and Dustin did it in several months. The product needs to speak to the needs of its users and gain their trust. Facebook

---

120 http://mogmaar.blogspot.com/2006/06/facebook-with-chinese-characteristics.html

121 http://mobile.gigaom.com/2006/08/18/airg/

122 http://software.gigaom.com/2006/07/27/cyworld/

I've found something to put here. Now it's your turn.

is now, in English, at (only) the most prestigious colleges in India. Technically, it would be very easy to localize the site to any language. I guess Facebook is trying to center its focus. That day will come, but will it come soon enough, or will a local competitor dominate? Will it be you, either with a vertical or regional adaptation, with a local twist?

Not Everything. Anything.

No, you can't do Everything. I said Anything.

So, now that I've excited you about your own potential and you're ready to run out and fix the world using only your bare hands and the Internet, I have a few words of ice water to drop on your head.

Our main human limitation is that we each have at most about eighteen hours a day for maybe thirty to forty years if we are lucky. If you choose the blessing of having children, one third of that is spent with a small, purportedly human, creature hanging onto your leg. We spend between fifteen and thirty years just getting ready, figuring things out, building out our personal social networks, and beginning to understand money.

The world may also constrain us. Are we running out of power? The blog of a major Southern California Web hosting provider, Dreamhost, <u>describes a sustained many day</u>

Go do. Build your idea. Share for help.

outage,[123] partly due to an unreliable supply of power. Google, Yahoo, and Microsoft are each building computer centers near the cheap and reliable hydroelectric power of the Columbia River on the Washington/Oregon border. Would VC and IPO money dry up with a potential sustained recession? On the other hand, whatever tremendous challenges arise, unless they destroy our civilization, will carry a need for Internet work, because whatever the solution is, it will involve better communication and coordination among peoples.

There is also only so much human attention, and it tends to clump. And as so much human attention is wasted on just attending, it's even harder to get anyone to meaningfully do something, whether it's for themselves or for you.

Even great people usually only did a few great things. So we need to choose carefully what that great Anything will be.

Lack of focus means your power is divided. You will lose any race if you are trying to juggle at the same time. Your superior talent can only take you so far. The only reason to divide your focus is if synergy among any two efforts will have greater power than either piece alone. Otherwise you'd be better off finding a greater vision for either one of the two pieces, and just forgetting about the other one. Don't just lower the priority of that other piece so it continues to take up valuable

---

123 http://blog.dreamhost.com/2006/08/01/anatomy-of-an-ongoing-disaster/

I've found something to put here. Now it's your turn.

space in your deeper mind. Instead, actually cut it away, as in "that would be great, but I'm not going to do it."[124]

Anything great is overwhelming, so breaking it down into small steps helps, as if it is actually a staircase that you are building and not a treadmill. You can trust that help will come in a way that exactly matches your passion. Perhaps it will be someone like Sean walking by your house without a clear place to stay.

Keep your focus and passion on a single, even if complex, vision. If it's a complex vision, you must concentrate your passion on a simple initial piece of it and start running with that.

If you don't have a vision yet, meditation, a realistic idol/role model/mentor, time for deep, creative conversations, topical and inspirational reading, and other things can help. But maybe you are just not ready for your journey yet. A vision can take time to find.[125] Be patient, but remember that you won't get far without one.

---

124 If reading that pissed you off as much as writing it did, read it again. And again. Read it until the feeling fades and you can accept it as the truth. I'll need to read it—daily—until, somehow, someday, I can just naturally let go of 90 percent of the ideas or offers that I encounter that I won't be able to do anything about.

125 That's what the world needs! A site to help people find their vision and keep it! Yeah! Let me see, I could start on that right now! Um, no.

Go do. Build your idea. Share for help.

The Future of Social Networking

Quite simply, the future goes to what works. Facebook works, but let's explore some others. Social networks are emerging like mushrooms and earthworms after a rain. Many will be eaten, some will be trampled, and most will just live short lives before giving way to the next generation. "What works" means it has to immediately improve my life without much effort on my part and provide instant gratification. Conversely, it must not annoy me. Within the confines of my own hedonistic use, it must create more value for the community of users. If this benefit of community gains scale exponentially for small groups, the site will grow explosively. Lastly, it has to work financially for the site: the service can't be much more expensive to produce than the site is able to monetize.

Steve of Youtube? I'm talking to you about your genuinely useful site. What's that? Oh, I understand. You can't hear me because you are talking to Larry and Sergey right now about how you really are worth more than a billion dollars because you are so essential and widely used, showing 100 million videos a day, but that they need to buy you this month—no, actually, right now!—before the next bandwidth bill arrives, because if they don't Yahoo, Fox, or Viacom will. Congratulations, Steve! And after your amazing sixteen-month achievement, I'm glad you can say "It's still fun."

I've found something to put here. Now it's your turn.

Let's look at three similar, non-niche, social companies and see whether we can evaluate their likelihood of success. Lets look at Flock, BlueOrganizer, and Diigo, in the interesting order of decreasing user commitment required. Significantly, this is also in the order of increasing benefits of network scale. Alas, I show my hand.

Flickr, MySpace, and Facebook are the clear winners in explosive usage. Many other sites have a core set of dedicated niche users. We're looking at these others less to review specific implementations and more to understand the space and the future.

These three sites all share the ambition of creating community around the browsing experience, and integrating people's data streams from disparate Web sites, for the user's convenience and for their trusted friends to see. I personally see these ambitions as extremely important, and I can't overstate that they may be the short-term killer app of the Web 2.0 Internet.

Flock is a social web browser. I met the founders of Flock at their private party during OSCON 2005 in Portland, Oregon. I was walking to a rock climbing gym for a workout when I met the founder of Plone walking on the street and he disclosed to me the party's secret location. It wasn't meant to be a secret, but that explained why the venue only had about a dozen people in it. That was okay, though, because having a lot of people would have distracted the Flock dev team from

Go do. Build your idea. Share for help.

completing and publicly releasing the first beta version of Flock, during the party.

I must first disclose that I have a small financial interest in Flock's success. I have a "Get Flocked" t-shirt from that party and on the day it overtakes Internet Explorer, I will sell it for big bucks. At the party, I learned that the Mozilla Foundation gets a boatload of money from Google for making it the default start page. The amount is in the tens of million, and that there is significant political infighting over that windfall. I never found out about Flock's model for financial success.

Flock installs easily, and the initial integration with Flickr/PhotoBucket for photos is quite simple. After that, it seems to work much like Firefox, and my photo stream is at the top. On the site I have two hints of a committed global user community of something over a thousand installations, as counted on its "Map of Flockstars" and its "I Flock" button downloads. So what is my immediate personal benefit for using Flock? I'm not sure I'll ever find out. But at least I have enough motivation that I want to write about it and not look completely ignorant. But I, along with the rest of the Mozilla-go-kick-some-IE-ass fan club, wish them well.

As for BlueOrganizer, again I must disclose that I have a financial interest in its success. Amazingly, I was able to register blueorganizer.org weeks after the launch of the product, and a squatter from Wyoming took the blueorganizer.com domain four months ago. This doesn't give

I've found something to put here. Now it's <u>your turn</u>.

me much confidence in its likely marketing success. Did those guys just not think about it? Or were they so married to the color blue from their company name and their idea that it's an "organizer" that they committed to launch it even after they knew they couldn't take the dotcom address?

TechCrunch gave AdaptiveBlue a glowing review. BlueOrganizer's structured approach to user information accrues valuable benefits. The default restaurant and other commercial data that shows up in the big left panel from the moment I installed it is of such low quality and is so irrelevant to whatever my mission is in the main browser window, that I felt a strong urge to uninstall it. It is important to launch fast, but do it with a small feature set that is truly compelling, and don't force unready, non-useful features into early adoption. AdaptiveBlue probably knows that its default content is not useful, so it is showing it as an example of the great potential of the product.

Unless it immediately does something for me today, I (and everyone else) will not go through the trouble of adding content to make it useful to me tomorrow. BlueOrganizer displays its potential loudly, to cover for its immediate lack of any initial benefit. Here's a speculation about this form of service evolution: BlueOrganizer collects a map of my friends from the Facebook read-only API and all of our posts from every Web site imaginable, and display ranks them. In this way

Go do. Build your idea. Share for help.

it could become a personal publishing platform and friend news service.

Diigo installs easily, but has the initially annoying habit of preempting Firefox's double-click text selector. The advantages of scale most accrue when Diigo-based annotations become widespread enough to be the standard way of commenting on Web sites. Indeed, this "alternate" Web could be a fun and democratic alternative to a simple Web presence, allowing visitors to effectively write graffiti on the pages of disliked sites. Unfortunately, at this time all comments have equal standing whether they are interesting or crap, and whatever the credentials of the author or their relationship to me. Such useful ranking on metadata will come in time. As will spam. A spam comment I put up on the "what's new" core Diigo site page lived there for days.

The two most winning features of Diigo are, first, that it works on top of my current social bookmarking service (whether that's Furl, Del.icio.us, or something else) so easily that I can cross-post to multiple services to show my activity to all of my friends regardless of which one they are using. Unfortunately, it doesn't support Furl's category, ranking, or page clipping features, which I use heavily. Second, it allows me to markup or highlight pages and send them to others even if they are not registered with the service. So my highlights are visible publicly or just privately to anyone.

I've found something to put here. Now it's <u>your turn</u>.

Diigo's challenge is making sure that everyone new to the site can understand how they can immediately gain value, and getting them to just do that until they want to see more. Their front page tries. But maybe people just don't read. I didn't. I just got annoyed that it took over my text-highlight functionality to always show me a new Diigo menu. With Flickr or Facebook you use the site in reader mode before you are ever asked to do anything, and often the asking is done by your friends, not by the site. The Diigo service is far from easy to start using at this time. And if you kindly indulge me just this once, I'll put my red hat on[126] and say that I just don't like the word Diigo. I don't feel like Diigo'ing anything, or asking my friends to Diigo something, whatever that means. If the service helps users slide into use naturally, and if few share my visceral aversion, and thereby attain a critical mass, this product design will succeed to reach its lofty ambitions.

Like these three services, Facebook is *a prototypical Web 2.0 company*, and I can say this with complete confidence, because I will now conveniently redefine Web 2.0 to my own purposes just as every other typist is doing.[127] I can say that this social collaboration explosion is Web 2.0, therefore we are experiencing the very source of Internet evolution.

---

126 http://www.amazon.com/gp/explorer/0316178314/2/ref=pd_lpo_ase/104-7834768-7691925?

127 See http://www.oreillynet.com/pub/a/oreilly/tim/news/2005/09/30/what-is-web-20.html, http://paulgraham.com/web20.html, http://www.slate.com/id/2138951

Go do. Build your idea. Share for help.

For me the key feature of Web 2.0 is distributed community, since this is what the Internet can do better than a desktop application or a neighborhood potluck. With Ajax, scripting languages like PHP/Ruby/Python, application frameworks like PHP/Rails/CMS, and Web APIs from just about every major site like maps.google.com, new sites are now naturally built as fast prototypes that integrate existing sites and features. Facebook was born out of this soup, and it will thrive as long as it keeps riding that trend.

Facebook looks properly committed here with the release of its developer API, and immediate interest by over 1,000 developer-users[128] in the first four days. I don't understand the security model for protecting sensitive data beyond the threat of being shut down for abuse. Also, the valuable relationship data stays the property of Facebook, whereas some Web 2.0 definitions would prescribe a more distributed ownership responsibility, or one in which that ownership rests with the individual user. Anyway, the API may produce a flood of creativity like the Yahoo and Google APIs inspired.

Ajax (used, for example, on the Facebook NCAA March Madness brackets) is helpful to Web 2.0 because it makes it easy to interact with Web data services, which can be anywhere, including on your own site. Even plain old javascript is nice in that it speeds up the response back to the user,

128 http://www.facebook.com/group.php?gid=2205007948

I've found something to put here. Now it's your turn.

most noticeably in highly interactive applications, and javascript frameworks like prototype,[129] make such development easier. Facebook doesn't use prototype or any other frameworks, usually preferring to do all application engineering from scratch.

As noted earlier, Web 2.0 emerges as the task of building a site becomes easier, thus the field is bustling and crowded. Social bookmarking services like Furl and Del.icio.us let me keep forever what I've found on the Web, shows me what my friends are reading (which is usually much better than the daily news), and helps me find other people with similar interests so I can see what they are reading. Digg shows me what is important in the news, like Slashdot used to do with its team of editors. However, Digg is more open to popularity cliques and gaming because there is no concept of friends, networks, or groups.

Let's look at two other generalized social network competitors: wallop and multiply.

Wallop is Microsoft's entry into social networking, based on many years of advanced work by their huge R&D department. Rumors of it circulated for years. I'm grateful they gave me access right into their first private launch. I tried to figure out it, and while I must admit the all flash interface looks really slick, I don't know how to use it. I still don't know any of the

---

129 http://prototype.conio.netv

Go do. Build your idea. Share for help.

faces they show me as "others", and without any connection to anyone the available tools to listen to music or upload photos don't mean much to me. Alexa's 3-year chart shows an interesting trend of "boom" with PR and then drift away. This and Cisco's purchase of tribe.com represent big company attempts in the social networking space.

Multiply.com is an interesting competitor without a niche market, and it is slowly ascending toward the Alexa 500. It is succeeding because it focuses on "real-world networks" of friends. At this point, a lot of its users seem to have exactly one connection—themselves—but its vision is correct, and the site is seeing active development. Interestingly, Multiply has enabled users to categorize their friend relationships, a first step toward classifying which friends are closer or more important. On this point, Zuck has intentionally decided to collect Facts about how users know each other in the Facebook social map feature instead of letting users make classifications. Facebook intends to algorithmically compute relationship closeness based on Facts and site behavior, more accurately and with less trouble than if users had to maintain it themselves. Like Facebook and MySpace, though, Multiply wants to own the user by providing more and more features (blogs, photos, videos) all locked within the small pond of its own site. A Web 2.0 trajectory would predict more cross-site integration, connections that appear natural to users rather than those indicated by company executive-planned corporate mergers.

I've found something to put here. Now it's your turn.

Nevertheless, Facebook is the clear leader in the serious social network game,[130] and it has an ambitious plan. The lead and momentum are with Facebook.

Facebook is coming out of its summer lull and, with the new freshman class infusion, should be approaching 10,000,000 members. Facebook's adoption rate with the 2006 incoming freshman class is as amazingly high as ever,[131] with about 90 percent of the target audience signing up for and heavily using the service. While both Bebo.com (with about 25 million) and MySpace.com (about 70 million) claim many more members, the real question for a social networking site is how many active users the site has, and how much the site has become an integral part of those users' lives. Of those 10 million Facebook members, over two-thirds typically visit the site every day. Over 90 percent of users who have ever signed up continue to use the site today. MySpace and Bebo did not release their numbers to me, but I doubt they are as strong. This tells me that Facebook *works* for users who try it.

---

130 MySpace is the leader in pageviews and membership. but as an open network, I don't think (smart) people really feel they can be themselves. I suspect they, like me, are less genuine or serious on MySpace. I don't have evidence for this, but consider this—a Facebook profile is tied to a single email address so it is inherently valuable. With MySpace you can always start again. I'd bet you, again without evidence, that many of those millions of members are in fact multiple accounts held by single individuals.

131 http://chimprawk.blogspot.com/2006/07/adopting-facebook-comparative-analysis.html

---

Will Facebook work for non-college users? Will it continue to work better for college students than any other site? Every large, successful Web site has a powerful vision of service. Google, eBay, and Yahoo all started with a simple, powerful vision on which they executed to a very high level of completion. Having a simple story, and executing it well, is also a great for attracting buyers, as PayPal and Overture have demonstrated.

Facebook has a big vision, but it is quite complicated. First I'll present several other big corporate visions, so we can appreciate how much more difficult and complex is Facebook's ultimate aim.

Google's big vision—to enable people to find stuff on the Internet—is clearly the most important and challenging task on the Internet today. I had heard during Google's early days that the company's goal was to make finding any information on the Internet easier than finding it on your own desk. Well, now with everyone's desk becoming clear and simple,[132] they'll need a new metaphor. Best estimates say the search game is in its second or third inning. There are more opportunities, but Google's success has come from how far it has progressed toward its vision.

---

132 http://www.amazon.com/exec/obidos/ASIN/0071433864/ ptradescom-20

I've found something to put here. Now it's your turn.

Yahoo's vision, which I've never seen clearly articulated, is, I think, to be everything to everyone, so that anything one wants to do a lot on the Internet can be done through Yahoo. Even in Japan, guess who[133] helped me plan my train itinerary, and my friend is running her small Japanese candle business[134] on the Japanese Yahoo network.

Microsoft dreamed of putting a PC on everyone's desk and could maybe have gotten something really big with achieving that, except for the small detail that people now see that we don't want a Windows PC on every desk. We'd rather have an iPod in our ears synced to a laptop, which is also tied to a phone device and plays games on our LCD TV. All all key services in the computer are enabled by remote Linux-based servers, which are maintained by someone else so that we don't have to worry about the nuts and bolts.

Oracle and Sun may have failed at their network computing attempts because it wasn't their fundamental vision and passion, but Yahoo and Google are certainly fulfilling the prophesy. Apple is more like Sony in that it can design any kind of consumer device—as long as it's really cool. The media-savvy iPod came about because Steve Jobs is a marketing guy with a foot in both the entertainment and technology worlds.

---

133 http://transit.yahoo.co.jp

134 http://www.geocities.jp/rassoku/index.html

Go do. Build your idea. Share for help.

Google is especially enthralled with the vision thing: "digitize all printed books," "replace email, IM, and the telephone with Gmail," "automate contextual Internet text advertising." It is easier to have a vision about something that already exists or is undeniably essential, such as a renewable, carbon-neutral alternative to fossil fuels. A vision isn't enough, of course. Others could execute the vision better, or the vision could be a threat to someone more powerful than you, someone who will play Godzilla to your Bambi.[135] Nevertheless, a grand vision seems to be a necessary if not a sufficient condition, at least until you are big and successful. (Like Microsoft, which can drift and dabble in whatever it wants until its Windows and Office cash-cows wander off to that big ranch in the sky.)

Amazon and Google are constantly evolving beyond their original visions, taking on new challenges and targets. How much should Facebook adjust and evolve? Which way would you like it to go?[136]

Facebook's Vision

Facebook's vision is both more complex and more ambitious, since Zuck aims to build something that didn't exist in the real world before. Facebook intends to improve the flow and

---

135 Don't miss this animated classic! (http://youtube.com/watch?v=BXCUBVS4kfQ)

136 http://www.fbbook.com/fblog/facebook-future

I've found something to put here. Now it's your turn.

quality of information shared between people, to actually improve communication and relationships. Facebook wants to broadly improve a fundamental human activity—and why not? It has succeeded in doing that for a broad swath of college-going Americans.

On the one hand, improving the means of communication isn't an unprecedented aim. The telegraph superseded the Pony Express. The telegraph yielded to the telephone. IM and VOIP are replacing mail/email and traditional telephone services. Communication methods are always improving, becoming faster, more reliable, and more expressive, that is, able to transport more information.

But these improvements have mostly been quantity-based improvements, such as delivery speed, reliability/security, price, and content throughput. VOIP, pretty much for free, can send billions of bytes per second of information across the United States, whereas Pony Express riders and horses could probably carry a pack of letters the same distance in a month. Back then, a correspondent might not have even known if her letter had arrived at its destination. Yet based on anecdotal evidence, the quality of communication probably hasn't improved much!

I suggested to Zuck that people[137] might want different profiles for different sets of friends, or at least for different circles, such as, say, their college buddies as opposed to their professional network. I got the impression that Zuck hopes Facebook will make such confused personal identities a thing of the past. After all, a majority of Facebook college alums continue to use Facebook every day, just as they did before graduating. Perhaps they can persist with a single coherent personal identify for years. Perhaps their old friends can keep them honest and true to their college selves, to their youthful dreams, and their new friends will be integrated into their existing groups. Perhaps they will find new friends who are more consistent with their college personality instead of being remolded to fit into a new circle of work friends whose character is very different from what they were in college.

Zuck, Dustin, and most of the Facebook engineers have succeeded at this. They've brought their college network and their college personality into their initial professional career, and I'm almost certain this would be everyone's ideal. For most of us, college was a superlatively fun and effective time in our lives. I bet we all feel that we learned and personally

---

137 Especially older, more complex, or more confused, people. I wouldn't want an ex-wife (if i had one), my kids, and my current professional friends to see the same profile. As Facebook opens to "work networks" and open-to-anyone geographical networks, the tension between current and former coworkers begins to emerge, as distinct from students and-alumni, since alumni are mostly happy, and colleges don't have "company secrets."

I've found something to put here. Now it's <u>your turn</u>.

grew to an astounding degree in those short years. Our working life doesn't always feel like that, especially if we become a new cog in a large corporate machine. We can go for years without growing much personally, and often we can come to measure our success by our bank account balance or by how much stuff we have accumulated.

Facebook doesn't have a MyStuff section even though having one would be an excellent business move. They may have it soon, because the stuff we have does communicate information about us. Perhaps college students may be less consumed by collecting stuff than older working folks, who soothe their weary souls by surrounding themselves with things. Or not, as perhaps a broad swath of America is overtaken by Affluenza.[138]

When do Internet users change, or when should companies adapt?

I told Zuck that older people display different personas to different groups of friends. And while he didn't tell me that was fake, not genuine, and uncool, he said it might not have happened to me if I'd had Facebook. I could've stayed genuine to myself, and communicated that coherently to all of my friends instead of just losing touch with them.

---

138 See http://en.wikipedia.org/wiki/Affluenza and http://www.affluenza.org/.

Go do. Build your idea. Share for help.

Yes, unlike the Facebook generation, I'm having a heck of a time tracking down my important college friends. My Japan trip was partly about that, since most of the old contact information I had was destroyed in a house fire three years ago. How quaint, eh? Yes, I wrote that stuff on paper. With a pen. Fortunately, Facebook is backed up against the loss to fire of your little book of contact information. Or of your cell phone to theft. Or of your laptop's hard drive to failure. You don't have to worry about these catastrophes as long as your important friends continue to value the network.

So Zuck seems to have solved the problem of immediately losing touch with your schoolmates by effectively enabling people to stay in loose touch over long distances. So when he sees some additional communication problem, it seems natural to him that Facebook can and will solve it. The solution is to build Facebook in a way that avoids the problem, and then the problem will no longer exist once everyone uses Facebook. Completely reasonable, right?

To look at the limits of how much people will adapt to use a product, contrasted with how much a product should evolve to serve its users, let's take another look at the "a person has multiple personas or profiles to show different people" issue. If real communication means that a person is genuine and real to everyone looking at his profile, then it means that he should have a single, consistent profile. Otherwise he is either lying or not revealing the full truth about himself, which is

I've found something to put here. Now it's <u>your turn</u>.

imperfect communication. So, if Facebook doesn't allow that, people will remain consistent among all of their online connections. Major social communication problem solved. Thank you again Facebook.

Maybe.

Will people alter their social behavior to better fit their new tools? Sometimes the answer is yes. Nowadays I and most technophiles loathe waiting days for a snail mail response, and have fully replaced personal letters with email. We may even be going digital with holiday and event cards, which would radically change their content.

Only if the social function is better served by the tool will it be adopted. IM seems preferable to email if the only criteria is speed and availability. IM has partially crashed, however, on the rocks of making users too available. In response, some IM clients now allow users to show a different status message to customizable groups of users while some IM users have resorted to always leaving their status as "busy" or "offline," contacting others only by initiating the conversation. Whereas talking during a phone call may be much faster than typing, IM creates a searchable record of the conversation[139] and allows me talk to more than one person about different things at the same time.

---

139 As a certain Republican congressman recently discovered.

Go do. Build your idea. Share for help.

So, does having a single persona result in better communication? Well, it is certainly simpler to maintain. Some would immediately invoke <u>Occam's Razor</u>[140] as proof that it is better.

On the other hand, what if human communication is naturally better when it is more complex? Maybe relationships will continue to be more complex than any tool created to manage them. I'm just a guy, so I never understand human relationships anyway.

Zuck, I'm told, has no material clutter in his life. He sleeps on a mattress on the floor, I think--though I haven't seen it and don't care to. He certainly has no clutter in the office. He has his small white iBook (like Aaron) and not much else. Aaron decorates his iBook with stickers but Zuck's is plain white, just like every single wall and piece of furniture in his "interrogation room," his closed office.

I speculate that Zuck has no need (at this time) for material stuff because his life is filled with Facebook. He is satisfied. Busy executives know that whatever is stacked into piles will never be used. This is also true for everyone else. Engineers didn't used to be like this, though. I remember when you weren't a *real* engineer if you didn't have a shelf of O'Reilly books that you'd read and refer to regularly, piles of hardware that you'd built into a robot in your spare time, and technical

---

140 <u>http://en.wikipedia.org/wiki/Occam's_Razor</u>

I've found something to put here. Now it's <u>your turn</u>.

magazines and software that would show that you were hip deep in the flow of information. Nowadays, real engineers seem to have nothing on their desks. Even I am slowly abandoning paper. What happened?

Finally, smart people have reached and are coming to terms with[141] information overload. O'Reilly is turning to its Safari virtual bookshelf and a PDF distribution channel.[142] At Facebook, most engineers have empty desks or just a few notes that are soon thrown away. I wonder if they've really simplified, or has the clutter just moved online, onto virtual desktops covered with icons, and onto thousands of backend servers.

Clutter is bad whether it is on a desk, on your laptop's desktop, or spread throughout the Internet. Having 500 friends is clutter. Having overlapping unconnected friends on five social networks is clutter. But good, rich complexity isn't always the same as clutter. It's okay to have your photos on Flickr, your videos on YouTube, and your personal information on your own Yahoo-hosted Web site because each one is better and cheaper at its core service. It's okay to go to several search engines when looking for something because they

---

141 I'm coming! Wait up! If I can do it, anyone can. When I was on the high school debate team, I had to cart around ten boxes of paper evidence. Even after a house fire taught me that "stuff doesn't really matter," I'm re-reading How to Simplify your Life (a great book) and again clearing off my desk.

142 http://www.oreilly.com/store/series/sc.html

Go do. Build your idea. Share for help.

really are different, and diversity is good. A Google-only world would really suck, just as a Microsoft only world came very close to sucking. As social networks move into more vertical niches, with specialized tools and features for each one, you may find that your Internet social life has become complex. But while having the same information in five different social networks is clutter, I predict that successful social networks will collaborate.

How do we deal with the reality of "friend clutter"? In the real world, we do it by ignoring people. I resolved my college friend clutter by losing touch with everyone from college. In many ways that's sad. But I get by. Will I do that again with my current circle of friends that happens to be centered around my kids' school? Do I do that every time I change jobs? Or with my church community every time I leave? Is this why Americans have so few deep, lifelong friendships? Is this just an American affliction or is the natural condition of Homo Modernus? In Japan as well, as people lose their rural connection to place and their lifelong employment connection to company, the enduring friendships that everyone once had and had taken for granted are weakening.

Facebook ensures (as long as people use it) that we'll never lose touch with our old friends. In my case, they'll just stay at the bottom of my 500-person-deep friends list, and Facebook will use its fancy algorithms to figure out what information I

I've found something to put here. Now it's your turn.

care about within that huge mash of activity among my 500 friends.

However, having a pile of 500 anything is clutter. On Google, I have a pile of billions of items, but I never have to see it because Google only shows me a beautifully simple box that fulfills all my wishes. With Gmail, Google is trying to do that for me with email. The "archive" button means "don't worry son, just let go." Today on Facebook I can't archive my friends, and it would be rude, sad, and maybe wasteful to delete them. So, even if I don't care about them anymore, if somebody updates their profile every day they will rise to the top of "MyFriends."

On LinkedIn I have 270 connections, all of people I really know. On Facebook I have almost a hundred. I have at least 100 to 200 friends and acquaintances who aren't on any social network yet. I need help organizing this clutter! The main online strategies I see among the people I know are "respond when contacted," "contact when you need something," "find interesting person to chat with when bored," and (years ago) "bond with my target hot chick and all friends of this hot chick." These strategies don't scale, are not especially nice, and probably wouldn't really get me what I most want in life. If I used Facebook heavily, I'd lose touch with people who are not on the system even if they are more interesting or important, just like I have a hard time staying in touch with friends who don't use email.

Go do. Build your idea. Share for help.

Currently, social networks have really been successful in niche
social segments, with MySpace comprised of the overlap of the
music/entertainment, youth, and <u>sex-driven</u> segments.[143]
MySpace is an open network wherein any member can see and
befriend any other member. This fact permits the overlap to
exist. Otherwise, members from different segments
presumably ignore each other. Closed networks like Facebook
serve their target segments very well, and need to figure out
the cross-network overlap, both on its own site and across the
Internet.

---

143 See <u>http://gigaom.com/2006/02/06/sex-crimes-and-myspace/</u>. I
just received this email: "You have been invited to join a MySpace
Group!" I open it and read, "Hi K, You have been invited to join the sexy
live webcams room group on MySpace." Ooo, lucky me! I click on the
link and, dang it, I get a "Server too busy" error. But that's okay because
I get an invitation like this just about every other day. Because it's
vigorously fought, this type of spam is almost never seen on Facebook.
In contrast, it's just about my only communication from MySpace.

I've found something to put here. Now it's <u>your turn</u>.

Go do. Build your idea. Share for help.

Your Future

No, first my future. I'm a megalomaniac so I can write anything I want in here. What have I done so far in my three decades of life? Not much. But I have read my own book, and I see the tremendous potential of these ideas. I'm joining a new startup—mEgo.com—and building something beautiful, I hope. This book isn't just a tabloid meant to dish the dirt on Zuck and other Facebook personalities. It's meant to empower you (and to remind me) to emulate them, with inspiration and a mix of ideas on business and technology. I'd like to start a discussion among all who read this book that will help propel us toward our own greatness. I'll write more if it feeds that goal.

The Internet has given us all incredible power. How will you use it? What's your passionate vision? Can you leverage your online or offline social networks to launch you?

If you are a parent, teach young people about good uses of the Internet and social technology (such as building a billion dollar company with it) and understand when young people use it differently.

If you are a technology professional, I hope that you might benefit by recovering your youthful ambition and inspiration. I address you all as young students now, whatever age and in whatever situation you are in. We can all share the youthful

I've found something to put here. Now it's <u>your turn</u>.

drive and ambition that propelled Facebook to its amazing heights.

The world is waiting for your inventions. It may be distracted looking at all the hot guys and girls wherever they happen to be, but, seriously, it is waiting for you. It will respond if you can break through that noise.

I said that you can do *anything*, not *everything*. And I said *you*. Yes, you. Everyone. Each of us.

Generation Debt: Why Now Is a Terrible Time to Be Young,[144] written by a twenty-four year old, has important data, a correct policy perspective, but a terrible subtitle and an even worse tone. I feel like crying in frustration and sympathy when I read about hopeless young men and women, trapped by debt, exhaustion, and inertia in low paying jobs, unable to see a better future, and clinging to regrets and blame. It is indeed a terrible time to be hopelessly in debt, and certainly kids growing up in the '50s and '60s had it easier. Certainly older and more powerful folks (much older than me) have stacked the deck in favor of themselves. But, dammit, Facebook shows us that we don't have to give in to that negativity. Don't give in.

---

144 http://www.amazon.com/exec/obidos/ASIN/1594489076/ptradescom-20

Go do. Build your idea. Share for help.

When I graduated, I was such a financial idiot that I put myself a few hundred bucks short of $100K into debt. I sat there— unemployed, without my part of the rent in my checking account, and holding over half-a-dozen maxed out credit cards. I turned it around,[145] and you can do, too, even faster and better. Read _Your Money or Your Life_.[146] Then be grateful. You have online tools and opportunities that I didn't, and you are smarter than me. The two things I did right were that I stopped spending money and always, continuously, obsessively, and passionately kept developing and evolving whatever I thought might be useful skills. Indulge me as I rephrase those two items.

1. Stop whatever you are obviously screwing up. Stop digging the hole in which you are standing. First stop spending money, the big items first. Then eliminate your blocks; remove your cement shoes. A genuine positive attitude, based on absolute and unconditional gratitude, is worth a million times

---

145 It's a long story, obviously. Catch, me sometime on my back deck at 2 a.m. by the light of the full moon overlooking the beautiful, oak-covered California hills when I'm tired of coding but not ready for sleep. The best book available is Your Money or Your Life, which carefully teaches that not only do you not need that X (whatever it is) but also that it's costing you Y hours of your life. The tools in it were literally priceless and life-changing. The only outdated bit is its advice to buy bonds. Don't do that. See? You have it harder and you'll need to be creative. Of all the books I've mentioned here, the most important one to buy is Your Money or Your Life.

146 http://www.amazon.com/exec/obidos/ASIN/1594489076/ptradescom-20

I've found something to put here. Now it's your turn.

its weight in gold. Just weigh it and see. Seriously, I am grateful for whatever happens, because I know it is for the best, for my future. I even felt that way about my house burning down. If nobody buys or reads this book then that is because it sucked, and thank God nobody saw it. Finally, any addictions must go. Obvious ones like drugs, alcohol, and gambling are relatively easy. Then continue on to snap thrillseeking, unsatisfying sex, pointless Web surfing, collecting this or that, and whatever else takes up your time without putting you ahead and giving you any long-term value.

2. Passionately do good things for yourself. Figure out something you are good at and then uncover what you need to do—today—to be better. Repeat. Persist. Whatever you try your best at, if it is good for people, it will be a valuable stepping stone. Luck always favors the prepared. So prepare yourself to be lucky.

What to do? What skills have value? What jobs are likely to be around in ten or twenty years so that your first (or next) steps toward a (new) career pay the highest dividends? What are people likely to need? Especially those who are likely to be rich, powerful, respected, or skilled at that time, the people who will be closest to you to serve! (These may be a very different groups of people than they are today.)

Friends and community are critical to your success. Do you have the right people around you? Facebook can help you here, as long as you are an active creator with whatever tools

Go do. Build your idea. Share for help.

you have. Surfing endless profiles and photos doesn't move your life forward.

Your attitude determines your opportunities. The economy for you is what you personally think it is. Whether you believe you will succeed or fail, you'll be right. Abraham Lincoln said, "Most folks are about as happy as they make up their minds to be."

Facebook, Dell, and Microsoft were founded by college dropouts. Google wasn't and I personally don't recommend it. Zuck and Dustin were just ready to move ahead, that's why it worked for them. Most people are not ready to give their entire heart, soul, and eighteen-to-twenty hours per day to an idea, or don't have that idea available to them.

Give that same passion to something while finishing your degree. Those somethings will be your ticket, as Japanese was for me. Drop *in*. Don't just go along with what advisors say, merely being satisfied to complete your English, Something Studies, Psychology, or Business degree, and suddenly realize that you don't know what to do with it. Study agriculture because you want to be a farmer, or biology because you are passionate about nano-bio-tech, or math because you want to compute better climate models to save us from global warming.

Drop *in* with passion in your studies. Don't just major in Business; *do* business. Don't just major in Creative Writing;

I've found something to put here. Now it's <u>your turn</u>.

publish some creative writing. Skills-based majors are wise because they keep your options open and are usually harder. In the realm of learning and personal growth, if it's easy it's likely that it's also not very valuable.

Drop *in.*

Now.[147]

---

147 http://www.fbbook.com/fblog/commit

Go do. Build your idea. Share for help.

Acknowledgments

Thank you, sincerely, for reading this book. It was a major investment of your precious time, and nothing gives an author more joy than your thoughtful attention. Now go use it!

I hope you received more than you anticipated, and I would love to hear your feedback (what you liked, what could be better, what you'd want added, anything) as well as your Facebook stories. If you have a startup idea, or want to participate in something with me, please introduce yourself. Contact me at karel@fbbook.com

Living the Facebook dream for a year was an unparalleled experience. Thanks to Mark Zuckerberg and Dustin Moskovitz for making it possible. Facebook tells me that I have about sixty-five friends within the company, and every one of them made my year wonderful, teaching me about life and technology and sharing countless special moments. Thanks especially to Kent, Nico, Paul, Ezra, Matt, Scott, Ditka, Nick, Amy (yay, someone with kids!), Naomi, Doug, Peter, Taner, Dan, Chris, Victor, Charlie, Dan, Jordan, Lucas, Shire, Paul, Jocelyne, Monica, James, Jeff, Ruchi, Christopher, Adam x2, Gilles, Susie, Sonja, Aaron, Areg, Bryan, James, Steve Chen, Grimm, Slee, Boz/Bob/Fet (that's TrahAn, everyone) spies of the Evil Empire, Shane, and Aditya.

I've found something to put here. Now it's your turn.

Thanks to my good friends Mark, Noah, Andre, Chris Fillius, Dave, Switzerland, and many other kind folks for reading early drafts and providing invaluable input. Michael leaped in from Pennsylvania, winning the cover creation contest and doing amazing design work. After enough people complained about the lack of editing, I begged Barry to help make this book more readable. He did masterful work, right down to this very sentence.

Writing a book and finding people to read it are two very different propositions. It is only due to the talents and efforts of Ted and Ryan and some others who must remain nameless, did you find this sentence among the plethora of quality content on the Internet.

This book would not exist without my wife Naoko, who liked the initial idea better than I did, kept me focused on it, and created time for me to write it. My dad inspired me by writing about twenty books himself and by providing timely encouragement. My daughters Mimoli and Elin also helped by providing background noise and by occasionally playing with my laptop.

Go do. Build your idea. Share for help.

Recommended Reading

Why

Generation Debt - why entrepreneuring is hard & so important.

Your Money or Your Life - why the frugality part is easy.

How to Simplify Your Life - why this attitude applies to everything.

What

An Inconvenient Truth - yes kids, in our lifetime.

Crashing the Gate - but not if we take over.

The Perfect Store - a great business can be built from idealism.

Hackers and Painters - by people like us.

How

Getting Real - get it.

Art of the Start - practical, fun howto, with the right attitude.

Small is the New Big - you're good enough, small enough, and gosh darn it, people like you.

Six Thinking Hats - think effectively.

I've found something to put here. Now it's your turn.

About the Author

Mr. Baloun architects and implements internet social applications. Most recently at Facebook.com, Mr. Baloun architected and managed development of site components as the first senior software engineer. His recent book "Inside Facebook" at fbbook.com, documents the industry.

Prior to his work at Facebook, Mr. Baloun architected and lead development of the templating engine that still serves all of looksmart.com and findarticles.com. Fluent in Japanese, Mr. Baloun co-developed a Java wireless information server, and led trial installations at Toshiba and NTT Docomo. An entrepreneur, Mr. Baloun has created a full featured commodity trading community site at ptrades.com, and is actively pursuing other interests (really). Mr. Baloun holds a Masters in Social Psychology from UC Santa Cruz.

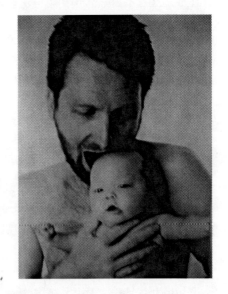

When not typing, Karel loves nature, yoga, occasional marathons, travel with his family, and email from readers: karel@fbbook.com.

Colophon

Colophon[148] is old Latin for cellophane[149], because this is what books used to be wrapped in before everything became digital. Usually reserved for dry information such as typefaces, I'll bring it to life with a question: want an index?

Me too. Since this book was made with iWork Pages '06 on a MacBookPro, and exported to PDF with Pages, in mostly Lucida Sans font, I'd hope enough people request Apple add indexing to this software package. Real writers, please tell me how this is usually done.

Lucida Sans is the sans serif complement to Lucida, designed by Kris Holmes and Charles Bigelow in 1985. The strong shapes and generous proportions are based on traditional Roman letterforms, making them clear and easy to read [...], as well as clean and powerful in business correspondence and newsletters. [150] Wow, did you know that?

The dead trees edition would be on 100% post consumer recycled paper, if only I/you could find a publisher willing to do that for me, on a book that is already being sold in digital format.

---

148 http://en.wikipedia.org/wiki/Colophon_(publishing)

149 http://en.wikipedia.org/wiki/Cellophane

150 http://www.adobe.com/type/browser/P/P_048.html

I've found something to put here. Now it's your turn.

9 781425 113001